G000094906

The Curious Incident of the Dog in the Night-Time (stage adaptation) GCSE Student Guide

Methuen Drama publications for GCSE students

Available and forthcoming

GCSE Student Editions

Willy Russell's *Blood Brothers*
Simon Stephens's *The Curious Incident of the Dog in the Night-Time*,
    adapted from the novel by Mark Haddon
Charlotte Keatley's *My Mother Said I Never Should*
Shelagh Delaney's *A Taste of Honey*

GCSE Student Guides

Willy Russell's *Blood Brothers* by Ros Merkin
Simon Stephens's *The Curious Incident of the Dog in the Night-Time* by
    Jacqueline Bolton, adapted from the novel by Mark Haddon
Dennis Kelly's *DNA* by Maggie Inchley
Alan Bennett's *The History Boys* by Steve Nicholson
J. B. Priestley's *An Inspector Calls* by Philip Roberts
R. C. Sherriff's *Journey's End* by Andrew Maunder
Charlotte Keatley's *My Mother Said I Never Should*
    by Sophie Bush
Shelagh Delaney's *A Taste of Honey* by Kate Whittaker

The Curious Incident of the Dog in the Night-Time (stage adaptation) GCSE Student Guide

JACQUELINE BOLTON

Series Editor: Jenny Stevens

Bloomsbury Methuen Drama
An imprint of Bloomsbury Publishing Plc

B L O O M S B U R Y
LONDON · OXFORD · NEW YORK · NEW DELHI · SYDNEY

Bloomsbury Methuen Drama

An imprint of Bloomsbury Publishing Plc

Imprint previously known as Methuen Drama

50 Bedford Square	1385 Broadway
London	New York
WC1B 3DP	NY 10018
UK	USA

www.bloomsbury.com

BLOOMSBURY, METHUEN DRAMA and the Diana logo are trademarks of Bloomsbury Publishing Plc

First published 2016
Reprinted 2016, 2017

British Library Cataloguing-in-Publication Data
A catalogue record for this book is available from the British Library.

ISBN:	PB:	978-1-4742-4059-8
	ePDF:	978-1-4742-4060-4
	epub:	978-1-4742-4061-1

Library of Congress Cataloging-in-Publication Data
A catalog record for this book is available from the Library of Congress.

Series: GCSE Student Guides

Typeset by RefineCatch Limited, Bungay, Suffolk
Printed and bound in Great Britain

CONTENTS

CHAPTER ONE

The Play

Reading a play

In his introduction to *Plays: Three*, Simon Stephens suggests that 'there's something curious about reading a play'. He describes the process as combining 'the oddness and difficulty of reading an instruction manual with the work of imagination involved in reading a poem' (2011: viii).

What Stephens identifies here is that a play is not only a creative work of fiction, it is also *a set of instructions for performance*. When you read a play, you are not only asked to imagine characters and a story, you are also invited to imagine the theatrical event itself. When reading a play, you will notice that there are two different types of writing on the page: the *dialogue* spoken by characters and the *stage directions* which provide more information about what the characters do, how the dialogue should be spoken and where the scene takes place. Lines of dialogue are written to be spoken aloud by actors. Stage directions, which are always written in italics, are not meant to be spoken: they are guidelines for actors, directors and designers on how to bring the world of the play to life. The dialogue and the stage directions work together to create the story. While it may sometimes be tempting to skip over them, stage directions are there to help you imagine more fully what is happening in the scene: where it is set, when it is set and how the characters speak and behave towards one another. If you wish to enter into the imagination of the playwright, then you must carefully read *both* the dialogue and the stage directions to try and visualize how the play might look, sound and feel on a stage.

Reading this play

Perhaps the most important stage direction in *The Curious Incident of the Dog in the Night-Time* (which we shall refer to from now on simply as *Curious Incident*) occurs at the very beginning of the play-text, before the action has even begun:

> *Scenes run into one another without interruption regardless of alterations in space or time or chronology.* (29)[1]

Curious Incident is structured into Part One and Part Two, each of which contains many different episodes, or 'chunks of action', which follow one after the other. These episodes – some of which are very short, some of which cover several pages – are not formally divided into individual scenes (e.g. 'Act 1, Scene 2', or 'Act 2, Scene Five'): the action does not stop and start with the ending and beginning of each scene but is instead continuous. You will see in the script that sections of text are separated from one another by a couple of blank lines. These spaces indicate to the reader a change, or 'alteration', in time and location but these changes do not interrupt the constant flow of stage action. In order to capture this sense that scenes 'run into one another without interruption', the synopsis below will talk of episodes 'dissolving' or 'shifting' into one another.

---

[1] All page references are taken from Jacqueline Bolton (2016), *The Curious Incident of the Dog in the Night-Time*, GCSE Student Edition, London: Bloomsbury Methuen.

As the title itself suggests, at the core of *Curious Incident* is a detective story. It is appropriate, then, that piecing together the story from the script itself requires some detective work. There are three things that might be useful to bear in mind as you read this play:

(1) *The play contains a mixture of* narrated *action and* enacted *action*. This is most evident at the beginning of the play. Here, the dialogue is a mixture of narration, provided by Siobhan who is reading aloud from a book written by Christopher, and enactment, as we see Christopher discover a dead dog in his neighbour's garden. So when, for example, Siobhan says 'My name is Christopher John Francis Boone', she is not referring to herself but reading out what Christopher has written. Siobhan continues to read from Christopher's book throughout Part One, and this provides a commentary on the action that unfolds on stage.

(2) *Scenes can take place in different times and locations simultaneously*. The beginning of the play is again a good example of this: Christopher's discovery of Wellington seems to be happening 'here' and 'now'. At the same time, however, Siobhan is reading Christopher's account of it, so we know that this discovery has *already happened* within the context of the story. While Christopher discovers the dog in a garden at midnight, Siobhan reads the book at school during the daytime. The simultaneous existence of different locations and times recurs throughout the play.

(3) *Everything that happens in the play takes place in real time, on a real stage, before a real audience*. This may seem obvious to say but it can be easy to forget that what you are reading is not a novel but a work of theatre. While the story of *Curious Incident* ranges over many different locations and times, it can be helpful to remember that there is only one place and time that the play itself really occupies: the stage, and the moment in which it is performed.

Overview

A straightforward narrative synopsis cannot tell us everything we need to know when studying a play, because a play is defined by *how* its story is told as much as the story itself. The following overview summarizes the main narrative events of the play.

Part One

A dead dog lies in the middle of the stage. A large garden fork is sticking out of its side. (31)

The play opens with fifteen year-old Christopher Boone and his forty-two year-old neighbour Mrs Shears standing either side of a dog which has been killed with a garden fork. Without waiting for any explanation, Mrs Shears accuses Christopher of killing her dog, Wellington.

Christopher's teacher, Siobhan, reads aloud from what we will later discover is Christopher's book. As we watch Mrs Shears repeatedly order Christopher to 'get away from my dog' (31), Siobhan continues to read out Christopher's story: we find out that his full name is Christopher John Francis Boone and that he knows every prime number up to 7507.

Christopher reacts to Mrs Shears's shouting by curling up on the grass and 'groaning' (32). A policeman arrives and questions Christopher about what he is doing in Mrs Shears's garden. While Christopher answers truthfully, the policeman's repeated questioning further distresses Christopher and he curls up on the ground again. Exasperated, the policeman tries to lift up Christopher. Christopher, however, cannot bear to be touched: he screams and hits the policeman. Christopher is arrested for assaulting a police officer.

The scene dissolves as Siobhan reads more from Christopher's book. We learn that people are confusing to Christopher because he finds it difficult to interpret their facial expressions: 'Siobhan says that if you raise one eyebrow it can mean lots of different things. It can mean "I want to do sex with you"' (34). Siobhan breaks from reading his story to protest that she never used those words. 'Yes you did', Christopher retorts, 'on September 12th last year. At first break' (ibid.).

The action shifts to a police station where Christopher has been taken for hitting the policeman. Christopher empties his pockets and removes the laces from his shoes but refuses to remove his watch and screams when the Duty Sergeant attempts to take it from him. Ed, Christopher's father, arrives to collect Christopher. He does not hug his son – Christopher cannot bear to be touched even by his own father – but instead *holds his hand out in front of him with his fingers stretched* (36). Christopher does the same and *they touch fingers* (ibid.). Christopher doesn't tell his father how he came to be at the police station but how, on the drive to the station, he saw the Milky Way through the car window. Satisfied that Christopher was not involved in the incident with Wellington, the Duty Sergeant lets Christopher off with a caution.

Siobhan continues reading from Christopher's book. Another reason that Christopher finds people confusing is because they 'often talk using metaphors' (39). Christopher dislikes metaphors – 'imagining an apple in someone's eye doesn't have anything to do with liking someone a lot' (39) – and regards them as a type of lie. Christopher detests lies and lying.

On the way home from the police station, Ed tells Christopher that he must stay out of trouble. Christopher announces that he is going to find out who killed Wellington. Ed becomes angry and orders Christopher to 'leave it' (40).

In his book, Christopher explains that his mother died two years ago. He came home from school one day to find no one at home, so he found the spare key and let himself in. When his dad came home and discovered Christopher's mum wasn't there, he made some phone calls and went out. When he came back two and a half hours later, he told Christopher that his mum had been admitted to hospital.

This flashback scene dissolves and we are returned to the central narrative, the morning after Christopher discovered Wellington dead. At school, Christopher greets Siobhan with the news that today is a 'Good Day' because on his way there he saw four red cars in a row. He tells Siobhan that he is going to find out who killed Wellington, even though his father has told him not to. Siobhan tells Christopher that if his father has told him not to do something then perhaps he shouldn't do it. She suggests that instead he write a story about what happened the previous night. Christopher agrees and we realize that this is the book from which Siobhan was reading at the start of the play.

We return to the flashback from two years ago and witness the moment when Ed told Christopher that his mother had died from a heart attack. Christopher expresses no emotion and instead speculates on the medical cause of his mother's death, concluding that it was 'probably an aneurysm' (44).

The flashback again dissolves and we are returned to the day after Wellington's death. That evening, Christopher goes to Mrs Shears's house to tell her that he didn't kill Wellington and wants to find out who did. Mrs Shears tells Christopher that if he doesn't leave immediately she will call the police.

The action shifts to a scene between Christopher and Reverend Peters, a chaplain at Christopher's school. Questioned by Christopher as to where heaven is, the Reverend replies, somewhat vaguely, that it is in 'another kind of place altogether' (45). When further pressed by Christopher to explain exactly where God is, Reverend Peters makes an excuse and leaves.

That weekend, Christopher decides to pursue his detective work. Although he doesn't ordinarily talk to strangers, he summons up the courage to knock on the doors of his neighbours' houses to ask if they know who killed Wellington. He knocks on the door of Mrs Alexander's house, who is pleased that he has come to say hello. Mrs Alexander chats to Christopher and, as he won't 'go into other people's houses' (49), offers to bring out some lemon squash and biscuits. The length of time she takes, however, makes Christopher nervous – he becomes worried that she might be ringing the police – and so he walks away.

With Siobhan, Christopher tries to figure out the motivation of Wellington's killer. He reasons that it might have been to make Mrs Shears upset. The only person he knows who didn't like Mrs Shears is Mr Shears, who divorced her some years ago. Mr Shears thus becomes Christopher's 'Prime Suspect' (50).

Christopher would like to sit his A-Level Maths exam but Mrs Gascoyne, the Head teacher of Christopher's school, is reluctant to allow this. Ed, however, will not take no for an answer and eventually Mrs Gascoyne relents.

Ed has found out from Mrs Shears that Christopher spoke to her about Wellington and is angry with him. When Christopher says that he suspects it was Mr Shears who killed Wellington, Ed loses his temper and makes Christopher 'promise' that he will 'stop this ridiculous bloody detective game right now' (53). Christopher promises, but his thoughts leap away immediately into a fantasy about being an astronaut. He thinks he would make a very good astronaut because he is intelligent, knows a lot about machines and computers and likes being on his own in small spaces. He blissfully imagines being in a spacecraft with 'no one else near me for thousands and thousands of miles', where all he 'could see would be stars' (54). For Christopher, being an astronaut would be a 'Dream Come True' (55).

Christopher has promised his father that he will no longer investigate the mystery of 'Who Killed Wellington' and so tells Siobhan that his book is finished. Siobhan thinks he should be very proud of what he has written but Christopher doesn't think it is a 'proper book' because it doesn't have a 'proper ending' (ibid.): he never found out who killed Wellington. Siobhan gently replies that 'not all murders are solved' (56).

The next day, Christopher runs into Mrs Alexander and she asks him why he didn't wait for her to return with the biscuits the other day. Christopher tells her, truthfully, that he was afraid she might ring the police and he would get in trouble again. Mrs Alexander chats amiably with Christopher: she is impressed that Christopher is going to take A-Level Maths and remembers that he doesn't like the colour yellow. Christopher takes this opportunity to ask Mrs Alexander about Mr Shears. Mrs Alexander advises that it would be best not to ask questions about Mr Shears as Christopher's dad would 'obviously [. . .] find it quite upsetting' (58). Christopher doesn't understand why his dad would find it upsetting and, in an attempt to make sense of why his father doesn't like Mr Shears, asks Mrs Alexander: 'Did Mr Shears kill Mother?' (ibid.). Mrs Alexander hastily reassures Christopher that this is not the case and expresses her condolences. She realizes that she has said too much and that she must explain herself. She makes Christopher promise not to tell his father what she is about to tell him, and reveals that, before she died, Christopher's mother had an affair with Mr Shears. Christopher's father will not want Christopher asking about Mr Shears, because it will 'bring back bad memories' (60). Christopher's reaction is to say that he should go now: 'I can't be on my own with you because you are a stranger' (ibid.).

Christopher arrives home from speaking with Mrs Alexander and manages to answer Ed's question about where he's been without telling any lies. Rhodri, a friend of Ed's, is there and fires a difficult maths question at Christopher. Christopher answers immediately but Rhodri admits that 'hasn't got a bloody clue' whether or not Christopher is right (61). When it comes to subjects like maths and science, Christopher is much more intelligent than the adults around him. As his conversation with Mrs Alexander evidences, however, Christopher finds understanding people and relationships and emotions much more challenging.

Here, the narrative briefly splits into three separate strands of action that take place simultaneously. Firstly, Siobhan, who is holding Christopher's book, asks Christopher if he is going to tell his father about the conversation with Mrs Alexander. Christopher, who has promised that he won't, says no. Secondly, Ed approaches Siobhan and holds his hand out for the book: '*After a short time*' the stage directions tell us '*she passes it to him*' (62). Ed '*begins reading Christopher's book*' – which up until now he didn't know existed (62). Siobhan then asks Christopher about his mother and he describes a time when he was nine years old and on holiday in Cornwall. Christopher remembers how his mother waded into the sea and said 'Bloody Nora, it's cold' (ibid.). On this line, a third strand of action emerges as the scene becomes a flashback featuring Christopher's mother, Judy. This flashback ends with Judy playfully fantasizing about what might have happened if she hadn't married Christopher's father.

Ed has read Christopher's book and is extremely angry with him. Although we have seen him lose his temper before, this time he is furious. From his point of view, he gave Christopher explicit instructions to stop his 'bloody ridiculous detective game' and Christopher has directly disobeyed him. Ed shouts at Christopher and, in a fit of rage, grabs him: Christopher screams at being touched and they fight one another, resulting in Christopher falling unconscious for a few seconds. Ed declares that he 'needs a drink' and leaves with Christopher's book (65): when he returns he is no longer holding it. Ed apologises for hitting Christopher and explains that he worries about him getting into trouble. He spreads his hand like a fan and Christopher accepts it: they touch fingertips. 'Where's my book?' Christopher asks, but he receives no answer from his father (65).

When he returns home from school the next day, Christopher searches the house in an attempt to find his book. In his father's bedroom he finds an old cardboard box. Inside this box is his book, together with lots and lots of letters which are all addressed to him. At this point, we hear his name and address spoken by his mother, Judy. He looks at the handwriting and notices that instead of dots over the letter 'i' there are little circles. He knows only three people who use circles rather than dots and one of them was his mother.

His dad arrives home and asks Christopher what he's been up to today. Christopher truthfully tells him about his day at school, but doesn't mention what he has just discovered. While Ed gets on with some DIY downstairs, Christopher goes to his bedroom and reads a letter that he took from the cardboard box. It is from his mother and in it she describes her new job, new flat and her life with 'Roger' – Mr Shears. She writes that she is sad Christopher hasn't written and hopes that he won't stay angry with her forever. Christopher observes that the postmark on the envelope is dated eighteen months after his mother died. He decides not to think about it anymore that night, as he doesn't have enough information and could easily 'leap to the wrong conclusions' (70).

It is raining heavily the next day and when Christopher returns home from school his dad, who is a plumber, has to go out on an emergency call. Christopher goes to his father's room and takes from the cardboard box the rest of the letters. There are forty-three in total and they are all addressed to Christopher. Judy appears and reads out the content of these letters while we watch Christopher *'assemble his train set'* (73). As the truth dawns on Christopher – that his mother is not dead but alive and living in London – his *'building becomes frantic'* (ibid.). Judy's letters reveal that she lacked the patience to deal with Christopher's sometimes aggressive behaviour when he was younger: 'I was not a very good mother, Christopher. Maybe if things had been different, maybe if you had been different, I might have been better at it. But that's just the way things turned out' (74). The difficulties Judy experienced with Christopher put pressure on Judy and Ed's marriage, leading them to argue constantly. Feeling lonely in her marriage, Judy started spending time with Mr Shears; they fell in love but she wouldn't leave because of Christopher. Then one day Christopher threw a chopping board and it broke Judy's toes. She couldn't walk properly so his father looked after him, and she noticed how much calmer Christopher seemed to be with his dad. She decided that Christopher and Ed didn't need her, and that it would be better for them all if she left. Christopher's father was very angry with her, called her selfish, and refused to allow her to say goodbye to Christopher.

The shock of these letters causes Christopher to roll into a ball and start *'hitting his hands and feet and head against the floor*' (75). He continues '*thrashing*' until it has '*exhausted him*' (77). Ed returns home to find Christopher lying in a pool of sick next to the box of his mother's letters. He realizes that Christopher has discovered the truth and clumsily attempts to explain. Christopher, however, doesn't respond. He doesn't react even when Ed touches him, so Ed gently cleans up Christopher, taking off his clothes and putting him to his bed. He tries again to explain and promises Christopher that from now on he is going to tell him the truth. He starts by confessing that it was he who killed Wellington. He explains that after Judy left, he and Mrs Shears became very good friends. Things between them had become strained, however, and they argued. After one particular argument Wellington seemed poised to attack, so Ed went at him with a garden fork. Having finally told Christopher the truth, Ed spreads his hand like a fan and holds it up for Christopher to touch, just like they did after their fight. Christopher, however, screams and pushes Ed backwards.

Christopher is convinced that because his father murdered Wellington, he could also murder him. His mind runs through all the options: he can't live with his father because that would be dangerous; he can't live with Siobhan because she is a teacher; he could live with his Uncle Terry but he doesn't like him and Mrs Alexander is a stranger. Finally, his mother's new address breaks into his thoughts: 451c Chapter Road, London NW2 5NG.

Part Two

Before we are returned to where the narrative left off at the end of Part One, there is a brief exchange between Siobhan and Christopher. Siobhan wants to know if Christopher would like to turn his book into a play. She thinks 'a lot of people would be interested' if 'people took your book and started acting bits out' (82). Christopher, however, does not want to make a play from his book: he dislikes acting 'because it is pretending that something is real when it is not really real at all so it is like a kind of lie' (ibid.). From this moment on, however, Christopher seems to develop a *meta-theatrical awareness* that he is in a play: he tells one actor that he is 'too old' to play the role of a policeman (83) and at points addresses the audience directly.

Christopher has decided to go to London to find his mother. This is the first time that Christopher has gone beyond the end of his street by himself and the prospect of making this journey is very frightening. He takes his father's debit card and, carrying his pet rat Toby, goes in search of the train station. A lady in the street points him in the general area but does not give him precise directions, so Christopher explains to the audience a formula for reaching places if you are lost (86).

At the train station, Christopher is physically overwhelmed by the visual noise of adverts, official signs, notices, labels, telephone numbers, warnings, instructions and posters that, because of his hypersensitivity to sights and sounds, clamour for his attention. Amidst the chaos, Siobhan 'appears' to Christopher and with her guidance Christopher safely navigates his way to the correct platform. On boarding the train, however, he is intercepted by the Station Policeman: Ed has reported his son missing and the policeman is to return Christopher to him. Christopher tries to run and screams when the policeman grabs him. Christopher refuses to leave the train and, as the pair tussle, it pulls out of the station with both of them on board. The policeman swears, and calls his colleagues to delay Christopher's father until they return.

Christopher reflects on how passengers on trains look out of the window but don't really notice anything. He, on the other hand, notices everything, down to the finest detail, which he lists for the audience (94). The sheer amount of visual and aural information that Christopher can absorb in any one moment means that sorting through and making sense of this information is very difficult: this is why busy places, such as the train stations at Swindon and London, confuse, overwhelm and tire him.

Christopher wets himself and the policeman sends him to the toilet. Instead of returning to his seat he climbs onto the luggage rack and crawls behind the suitcases. He is both hiding from the policeman and being on his own in a small space, which he likes. To comfort himself further, he counts through prime numbers. The policeman notices he is missing but fails to find him. People come to remove their bags from the luggage rack but they are too busy and self-involved to pay much attention to Christopher. The train finally arrives at Paddington Station, London.

Christopher asks a woman at the information desk for directions to his mum's house and she points him in the direction of the underground. Like Siobhan at Swindon train station, Ed 'appears' to Christopher and tries to persuade him to come home. Christopher replies that home is no longer Swindon, it is London. Unable to persuade him otherwise, Ed talks him through how to safely board an Underground train: 'Count the trains. Figure it out. Get the rhythm right. Train coming. Train stopped. Train going. Silence' (102–103). Suddenly, Christopher realizes that he has lost Toby, his pet rat. He spots him running along the tracks and climbs down onto the line, to the horror of other passengers waiting on the platform. A man manages to pull Christopher off the tracks but Christopher screams at him for being touched. A woman approaches Christopher to ask if he is alright but he threatens to cut off her fingers with his Swiss Army knife.

With Toby, Christopher boards the Underground train and eventually arrives at Willesden Junction. He buys an A–Z and finds his mother's house. Judy and Roger arrive home to find Christopher curled in a ball, exhausted, outside their flat. Judy rushes to hug him but Christopher pushes her away so hard that he falls over. She apologizes for forgetting, and instead spreads out her hand in a fan: they touch fingertips. Christopher tells his mother and Roger that he is coming to live with them because 'Father killed Wellington with a garden fork and I'm frightened of him' (107). Judy takes Christopher inside and gets him into bed. When she asks Christopher why he never wrote to her, he explains that his dad had told him she was dead. When Judy starts to 'howl' with anger and grief, Christopher simply asks 'Why are you doing that?'(108).

A policeman arrives to speak to Christopher but, as Judy is happy for him to stay, the policeman leaves them to their own devices. Later, Ed arrives from Swindon, demanding to talk to Judy. They argue, and Ed barges his way into Christopher's room, who brandishes his Swiss Army knife for protection. Ed apologizes and tries to get Christopher to touch fingertips with him. Christopher ignores him and starts groaning. The policeman returns to escort Ed from the house.

The next morning over breakfast, Judy and Roger argue over how long Christopher can stay: Judy is happy for it to be indefinite but Roger is not. Christopher announces that he has to return to Swindon to sit his A-Level Maths exam. Judy is impressed but does not want to commit to returning to Swindon with him: 'Let's talk about this some other time, OK?' (114).

Having taken two days off to look after Christopher, Judy has lost her job. Roger is unsympathetic, Ed is threatening to take her to court and Christopher is insisting that he return to Swindon to sit his Maths A-Level. Judy is struggling to keep on top of the situation and suggests that Christopher take his exam the following year. Christopher protests but later, when they are walking on Hampstead Heath, Judy tells him that she has arranged with Mrs Gascoyne to postpone his exam. This sends Christopher into a wild panic and he screams and screams.

Roger brings some science and maths books from the library but Christopher refuses to read them. Judy attempts to enforce a star-chart system to persuade Christopher to eat. Later, Roger comes into Christopher's room, very drunk. He swears and grabs at Christopher, who rolls himself into a ball and moans. Judy discovers them and pulls Roger away, apologizing profusely to Christopher.

In the middle of the night, Judy packs some clothes and tells Christopher to get into the car. She is leaving Roger and they are returning to Swindon. Christopher is scared about seeing his father but Judy reassures him that everything will be alright: Ed will stay with Rhodri until she and Christopher find somewhere new to live. Now that they are back in Swindon, Christopher once again asks his mother if he might sit his A-Level; his obsession with this exam continues to exasperate Judy.

The next day, Judy takes Christopher to his school and explains to Siobhan that Christopher 'won't eat' and 'won't sleep' because he wants to sit his A-Level (123). Siobhan confirms that Mrs Gascoyne still has the A-Level papers in sealed envelopes. Christopher tells Siobhan that he is very tired but still wants to sit the exam (122–123).

When he attempts the paper, however, Christopher panics and is unable to read the questions. Siobhan 'appears', just as she did at Swindon station, and tells him to stop groaning, catch his breath and 'count the cubes of cardinal numbers' in order to calm down (125). He does so and is soon able to answer a question: 'Show that a triangle with sides that can be written in the form $n^2 + 1$, $n^2 - 1$ and $2n$ (where n is greater than 1) is right-angled' (ibid.). Siobhan advises Christopher not to explain the answer to the audience – 'people won't want to hear about the answer to a maths question in a play' – but he protests that it's his 'favourite question' (ibid.). She suggests that he explain it after the show: that way, 'if anybody wants to find out how you solved the maths question then they can stay and you can tell them at the end' (125). Christopher agrees.

After the exam, Ed approaches his son to ask how it went. Encouraged by Judy, Christopher tells him. Ed thanks him and tells Christopher he is very proud.

Siobhan asks Christopher about the new accommodation he and his mother have moved into and he complains that he has to use the toilet with other people. He asks Siobhan whether he can come and live with her and she gently explains why this isn't possible: 'I'm not your mother, Christopher' (127). He tells her that, because his mum doesn't finish work until 5.30pm, he has to go to his dad's house after school. He pushes his bed up against the door and doesn't reply when his dad tries to talk to him.

One day, Ed sets a kitchen timer and begs Christopher for just five minutes of his time. He explains that he 'can't go on like this' and that he needs Christopher to learn how to trust him again (128). He calls it a 'project' that they will both work on together: Christopher will spend more time with Ed and Ed will prove to Christopher that he can be trusted. To show Christopher he means what he says, Ed gives him a present: a Golden Retriever puppy. Sandy, as Christopher names him, will live with Ed and Christopher can take him for walks whenever he likes.

Siobhan presents Christopher with his A-Level result: a grade A. Although his reaction doesn't reveal it, he says he is happy with the achievement: 'it is the best result' (129). He tells Siobhan that he is spending more time with his dad, who has told Mrs Gascoyne that Christopher will take A-Level Further Maths next year. Christopher is planning to go to university, where he will get a First-Class Honours degree and become a scientist. He believes he can achieve this because he has proved that he is 'brave': he went to London on his own; he solved the mystery of 'Who Killed Wellington'; he found his mother and he wrote a book (130). 'I know', Siobhan replies, 'we turned it into a play' (130).

Postscript/Maths Appendix

After the curtain call, just as Siobhan promised he could, Christopher reappears to explain how he solved his Maths A-Level question: 'Show that a triangle with sides that can be written in the form $n^2 + 1$, $n^2 - 1$ and $2n$ (where n is greater than 1) is right-angled'. He uses 'everything in the theatre' including lights, lasers, smoke machines, light-emitting diodes, speakers, projectors 'and a woman called a deputy stage manager who will operate these' (131) to show how he worked out the correct answer. In less than six minutes, Christopher demonstrates how he arrived at the solution: 'And that is how I got my A Grade!' (134)

Context

The novel

The Curious Incident of the Dog in the Night-Time is a novel by Mark Haddon, first published in 2003. It is written from the first-person perspective of a fifteen year-old boy, Christopher John Francis Boone, who is writing the book for a school project. Prompted by the discovery of a dead dog in his neighbour's garden, Christopher's attempts to find the murderer develop into a more complex journey of self-discovery. Although never explicitly stated, from Christopher's narration we understand that his behaviour – his difficulties with understanding emotions and reading people's faces; his dislike of being touched; his emotional detachment from the events around him; his obsessive detailing and explanations; his aptitude for maths and physics – is that of a teenager who is autistic. While the book that Christopher is writing focuses on solving the mystery of 'Who Killed Wellington', it becomes clear that the real subject of the novel by Mark Haddon is Christopher himself. *The Curious Incident of the Dog in the Night-Time* was an instant success with both adults and younger readers, selling over two million copies and winning the Whitbread Book of the Year and the *Guardian* Children's Fiction Prize.

Because of the book's success, Haddon received many offers from producers who wanted to adapt the book into a play. To begin with, Haddon had thought this 'a preposterous idea': how could a book 'set entirely in the head of single character' be transformed into theatre without doing the novel 'irreparable damage'? (Haddon, 2013). Eventually, however, he became curious as to how this might be done and approached the playwright Simon Stephens, a friend whose work he admired, to ask if he would like to adapt the novel for the stage. Stephens, who was already a fan of the book, accepted on condition that he wasn't paid for his initial work, thereby removing some of the pressure to succeed. With less pressure, Stephens was able to be more daring with his adaptation. This open and experimental approach has, arguably, been central to the play's subsequent success.

The play

Stephens's stage adaptation of *The Curious Incident of the Dog in the Night-Time* premiered at the National Theatre, London, on 2 August 2012, directed by Marianne Elliott with set design by Bunny Christie, lighting design by Paule Constable and choreography by Scott Graham and Steven Hoggett. It was enthusiastically received by audiences and critics, and transferred to the Apollo Theatre in London's West End in March 2013. In that year it won an incredible seven Olivier Awards (which recognize excellence in professional productions staged in London) including Best New Play, Best Director and Best Actor for Luke Treadaway's performance as Christopher.

In October 2014, the National Theatre production made its debut on Broadway, New York, at the Ethel Barrymore Theatre. The production opened to rave reviews and won a clutch of awards, including six Tony Awards (the US equivalent of Olivier Awards). These, once again, included Best Play, Best Direction of a Play and Best Actor in a Play, this time for Alex Sharp in the role of Christopher. In 2015, the National Theatre production embarked on a national tour, with Joshua Jenkins in the central role.

Stephens initially shared Haddon's uncertainty about adapting a novel 'told entirely through Christopher's perspective' for the 'three-dimensional medium of the stage' (Stephens, 2015). In Haddon's words, the challenge was how to 'tell the story from outside Christopher's head without losing something really important about his peculiar view of the world from inside it' (quoted in Bunyan and Moore, 2013: 127). The dramatic form does not enable us to get inside Christopher's head in the way that the novel permits; instead, we have to listen to what he says and does in order to work out what he is thinking and feeling. The same is true of the people around Christopher. We do not experience the characters of Siobhan, Ed, Judy and others through the filter of Christopher's mind but instead have to interpret the behaviour and actions of those characters ourselves. These characters 'are suddenly right there in front of us, as real as Christopher himself. Their words, their actions, their feelings now have equal weight. They affect us directly' (Haddon quoted in Bunyan and Moore, 2013: 127).

Aside from the necessary shift from the subjective 'first-person' viewpoint of the novel to the objective 'third-person' viewpoint of the stage, Stephens's adaptation is extremely faithful to the narrative, characters and environments described in Haddon's novel. While the action is condensed for effective story-telling, Christopher remains the central protagonist. Just like the novel, the play is created from the book that he writes: it is his story and his world that is created onstage.

Autism and Asperger Syndrome

Although Christopher's condition is never named in either the novel or the play, he does display behavioural traits associated with autism and, in early publications of the novel, is described on its cover as having Asperger's Syndrome. There is currently a debate in the medical and social care community over whether it is helpful to distinguish between autism and Asperger's; some prefer to identify Asperger's as simply a type of autism, while others argue that the difference is significant enough to merit two distinct diagnoses. While both terms relate to the same condition, the traditional use of the term Asperger's has applied to children and young people who, unlike others with autism, do not generally experience delays in early language development. On the contrary, they may be well ahead of their peers in some ways – reading at a very young age or talking like an adult before they have even started school.

Whether or not it is useful to distinguish between autism and Asperger's, both terms can be understood as a type of developmental disability, meaning that individuals may have problems developing intellectual, physical, learning, language and/or behavioural skills. Autism is a 'spectrum condition' which means that it can differ widely from person to person. This variation between individuals is sometimes referred to as being 'high-functioning' – able to lead relatively independent lives – or 'low-functioning' – requiring a great deal of support in many areas of life. These terms, however, are now seen as too simplistic by some in the autism community, as a so-called 'low-functioning' person may be extremely adept at certain things that a so-called 'high-functioning' person finds challenging. In short, autism is complex in how it affects different people and no two individuals with autism will face the same challenges.

According to Ambitious about Autism, a UK-based charity that campaigns to change policy and practice for children and young people with autism, the difficulties autism can create may be grouped into two main categories: *social communication/ interaction* and *repetitive behaviours and activities*.

Social communication/interaction

People with autism can find it very difficult to talk to and socialize with other people, often preferring to be by themselves. Understanding jokes, metaphors, sarcasm and other subtleties, such as hints or irony, can be difficult because they understand language literally (directly according to its proper meaning), not figuratively (alluding to something other than its 'proper meaning'); in the play, for example, Christopher explains his dislike of metaphors (39). People with autism may take instructions very literally; indeed, Christopher complains to Siobhan that 'people often say "Be quiet" but they don't tell you how long to be quiet for' (43).

People with Asperger's may have an excellent vocabulary but, as inflection and expression are socially learned, they can find it hard to manage the tone of their voice and so sound robotic or monotonous. People with autism can also have a tendency to speak in 'echolalia': the repetition of particular sounds, words or phrases simply for the satisfaction of saying them over and over, irrespective of whether the phrase is relevant to the situation. Phrases chosen by people with autism are often, though not always, picked up from recorded voices rather than ordinary conversation – from a favourite television show, for example, or automated announcements.

It is also often very hard for people with autism to read nonverbal cues, such as facial expressions and body language (Christopher finds people 'confusing' because they 'do a lot of talking without using any words' [34]). As a result, they can seem oblivious or callous – although in reality they have simply missed or misread the signals. People with autism are often described as 'lacking empathy' but this can be misunderstood. It is not necessarily that they can't 'feel' for, or empathize with, others but that autism interferes with the ability to both notice and interpret other people's feelings. This is a skill technically described as 'social imagination'. Even if a person with autism can tell what someone else is feeling, s/he may not know how to respond to them appropriately. Some people with Asperger's, however, may be entirely comfortable with themselves: their interests satisfy them and their difficulties do not interfere with anything they want to do, meaning that problems with social interaction may not feel like a serious loss.

Repetitive behaviours and activities

People with autism may be prone to developing rules and rituals; Christopher, for instance, believes that seeing four red cars in a row on the way to school makes it a 'Good Day' and that a Good Day is a day for 'projects and planning things' (42). Other rules might involve disliking particular colours, or refusing certain kinds of food because of its texture or colour (Christopher will not eat food that is yellow). People with autism can become attached to doing certain things the same way each time, and can get extremely upset if their routines are disturbed.

As well as being inclined to rules and rituals, it's common for a person with autism to have difficulty processing the information that their eyes, ears, nose, muscles and skin are sending to the brain. These sensory difficulties are basically a question of certain senses being either hypersensitive (oversensitive) or hyposensitive (under sensitive). If a sense is 'amplified' ('turned up') in a person with autism, they will be vulnerable to 'overstimulation' and may become physically and mentally overwhelmed (see Christopher's experiences at Swindon and Paddington Stations).

According to the Office of National Statistics, one in one hundred children is diagnosed with autism. Its cause is not known but is most likely to stem from the interaction of various factors: genetic, neurological and psychological. While many learn to manage the more stressful aspects of their condition and acclimatize to social rules, even the most independent people are still dealing with a complicated condition. Early intervention and the right help can be incredibly important. For more information on autism, including advice, support and links to related organizations, visit www.ambitiousaboutautism. org.uk.

A story about 'difference', not 'disability'

While it is useful and necessary to be informed about autism when engaging with *Curious Incident,* it is worth remembering Mark Haddon's assertion that his book is 'not a book about Asperger's [. . .] it's a novel about difference, about being an outsider, about seeing the world in a surprising or revealing way' (Haddon, 2009). By his own admission, Haddon conducted very little research into the condition because, for him, 'imagination always trumps research. I thought that if I could make Christopher real to me then he'd be real to readers' (ibid.). Similarly, when it came to adapting the novel for the stage, Stephens states that he did 'no research' for the character of Christopher at all: 'I just imagined him entirely from Mark's book' (Stephens, quoted in Ue, 2014: 116). It is important to remember that neither the novel nor the play provide a medically

authoritative reference guide to autism. Christopher is a
fictional character imagined by his authors so that we, as readers
and as spectators, might 'imagine other possibilities and explore
other [. . .] worlds' which might otherwise remain unfamiliar
and inaccessible to us (Stephens, 2011: viii).

Things to do

Think about these questions and discuss them in small
groups, or as a class:

1 Actor Luke Treadaway, who played Christopher in the
   original National Theatre production, claims that 'even if
   you're not like Christopher you can still find Christopher
   in yourself, or find yourself in Christopher' (Treadaway,
   2015).

   ● Do you agree with this statement?

   ● What aspects of Christopher do you recognize in
     yourself (for example, do you have superstitions, like
     not stepping on pavement cracks, or not walking over
     three drains in a row?)

   ● What aspects of Christopher's behaviour are more
     difficult to understand?

2 Read the opening page of Mark Haddon's novel (you can
   access this by using the 'Look inside' facility provided by
   online booksellers).

   ● What differences emerge from reading the opening of
     the novel alongside the opening of the play?

   ● How many differences between reading a play and
     reading a novel can you list?

3 Siobhan points out to Christopher, who doesn't trust
   stories because they are 'not really real', that 'some

people find things which are kind of true in things which are made up' (82).

- What do you think Siobhan means by 'true' in this sentence?
- Do you agree with Mark Haddon that 'imagination always trumps [beats, wins out over] research'?

Themes

Difference

Christopher's 'difference' manifests both in his social interaction with others and in the ways that he perceives and mathematically interprets the world: a playful example of this is when he asks Mrs Alexander whether by 'Battenberg' she means 'a long cake with a square cross-section which is divided into equally-sized, alternately coloured squares?' (49). He can conceptualize the expansion of the universe, the global scale of the water cycle and the molecular origins of life but he cannot eat yellow food, use a toilet that is not his own or understand other people's emotions. Whilst Christopher's mind is, in many respects, extraordinary, his behaviour can be extremely challenging, exasperating and, at times, frightening. The characters most keenly affected by Christopher's 'difference' are his parents, Ed and Judy Boone, whose marriage, as Judy's letters reveal, has broken down under the strain of caring for Christopher. Perhaps the most challenging aspect of Christopher's condition is his refusal to let them touch him in any way. Ed and Judy are denied the joy and pleasure of picking up, holding, cuddling or kissing their only child; the only way they are able to provide Christopher with comfort or reassurance is by holding out their hand and touching fingertips with him. In the words of Nicola Walker, who played Christopher's mother in the original production, what the character of Judy was 'looking for and not getting was that basic physical contact with her son, and that's what destroys her' (2015).

Curious Incident not only considers what it is to be 'different' but also depicts how others react when confronted with 'difference'. Unlike a physical disability, an individual's developmental disability cannot necessarily be perceived just by looking at them. Christopher looks like a teenage boy – almost a young adult – so when his behaviour imitates that of a child, the adults in the play typically mock him or become angry. The behaviour of these adults exposes the ignorance of which many of us, unfortunately, can be guilty when confronted with someone who we perceive as unfamiliar and 'different'. For Walker, *Curious Incident* is about:

> how you are treated when you do not behave in socially acceptable ways – and also about how we are all, all of us, somewhere on that scale. We all have to negotiate social norms; some of us are better at negotiating social norms than others and that is okay. If you enter into Christopher's world, you will have a far more successful relationship or conversation with him. If you try to contain him in something that is considered 'normal behaviour' it won't work. Yes, it is frightening when you don't understand someone but if you take the time to exist on their level it's far less frightening. (2015)

Walker's point that we are all on a 'scale' of conforming to reputedly 'normal' behaviour is important. Some of the play's most poignant – and gently comic – moments occur when adults recognize in themselves something of Christopher's world. When talking to Mrs Alexander, for example, Christopher states 'I don't like to go anywhere outside unless I'm on the school bus to school' and Mrs Alexander, a woman of advanced years, replies 'Yes, I know how you feel' (58). Similarly, when Christopher tells his dad about Joseph, 'who bangs his chin and screams a lot', Ed responds 'I know how he feels' (71). *Curious*

Incident asks us to reflect upon our own attitudes towards 'difference', to question 'common-sense' ways of seeing the world, and to recognize, value and exercise our ability (denied to Christopher) to *empathize* with the feelings and experiences of other people.

Things to do

1 'I see everything', Christopher tells us. 'Most other people are lazy. They never look at everything. They do what is called glancing, which is the same word for bumping off something and carrying on in almost the same direction' (93).

  ● Take a good look around your classroom. When you get home, make a list of everything that you remember about it: objects, materials, colours, the seating arrangements, etc.

  ● The next time you are in that classroom, compare your list with others. How much detail did you include? How much did you miss out?

2 Mrs Gascoyne is reluctant to let Christopher sit his A-Level Maths. She says they 'can't treat Christopher differently to any other student' and that allowing Christopher to take this exam 'would set a precedent' (51).

  ● What point is Mrs Gascoyne making here?

  ● Do you agree with her? In pairs, debate the arguments for and against letting Christopher sit the exam.

3 Read p. 57 *from* '**Voice One:** Customers seeking access to the car park . . .' *to* 'Dogs must be carried at all times'.

  ● Think about a public place that you visit regularly and think about how it might be experienced by Christopher. Dramatize your place, using Stephens's method of five voices.

Imagination and reality

Towards the end of Part One, when Ed discovers Christopher lying on the floor after reading his mother's letters, a short exchange between Christopher and Siobhan unexpectedly breaks into the scene. Siobhan is holding a tube of Smarties, and she asks Christopher what he thinks is in the tube:

Christopher   Smarties.

She opens it.

Siobhan   It's not Smarties. It's a pencil. If your Dad came in now, and we asked him what was inside the Smarties tube, what do you think he would say?

Christopher   A pencil. (78)

The Smarties Tube Test is an exercise often used by medical professionals to help diagnose autism. The exercise tests 'Theory of Mind', the name given to the ability to deduce how others are feeling, what their intentions are and what they are likely to know or not know. If Christopher possessed Theory of Mind, he would realize that his dad would also think there were Smarties inside the tube. He fails, however, to recognize that his father might think differently to him; unable to put aside his knowledge that in reality the tube contains a pencil, Christopher believes that his father would think the same.[2]

The Smarties test reveals that Christopher lacks 'social imagination'; that is, the empathetic ability to put himself in someone else's shoes. This is not to say, however, that Christopher does not possess any kind of imagination; indeed, part of what makes his mind so brilliant is his ability to imagine

---

[2] For more information see: 'The Smarties Tube Test Theory of Mind', *Blethers Speech and Language Therapy*, 9 September 2014 <http://edinburgh-lothian-mobile-speech-therapy.co.uk/news/the-smarties-tube-test-of-theory-of-mind/%E2%80%9D>

and describe the Milky Way, the solar system, Black Holes, red dwarfs and the expansion of the universe. He loves to imagine that he is an astronaut 'in a tiny spacecraft thousands and thousands of miles away from the surface of the earth':

> I would be able to look out of a little window [. . .] and know that there was no one else near me for thousands and thousands of miles which is what I sometimes pretend at night in the summer when I go and lie on the lawn and look up at the sky and I put my hands round the sides of my face so that I can't see the fence and the chimney and the washing line and I can pretend I'm in space. (54)

Christopher is capable of 'pretending' but his imagination is informed and inspired by scientific thought experiments and mathematical paradigms (established patterns or structures of thinking about the world). He makes sense of the world strictly through facts, logic and reason, which are far more tangible to him than emotions and feelings. Christopher is not, for example, sad to learn about his mother's affair with Mr Shears because 'Mother is dead and because Mr Shears isn't around any more. So I would be feeling sad about something that isn't real and didn't exist and that would be stupid' (62). Christopher is also comforted by his realist assessment of our relationship to the universe:

> When you look at the sky at night you know you are looking at stars which are hundreds and thousands of light years away from you [. . .] And that makes you seem very small, and if you have difficult things in your life it is nice to think that they are what is called negligible which means they are so small you don't have to take them into account when you are calculating something. (115)

The reason metaphors are confusing to Christopher is because he attempts to make literal sense of them: 'When I try to make a picture of the phrase in my head it just confuses me because imagining an apple in someone's eye doesn't have anything to do with liking someone a lot' (39). Because a metaphor is not factually 'real' (it is something described in terms of something else), for Christopher this means that it is not 'true' and, therefore, 'should be called a lie' (ibid.). Christopher reserves the same harsh judgement for acting, towards which he is intensely suspicious: 'I don't like acting because it is pretending that something is real when it is not really real at all so it is like a kind of lie' (82). What Christopher is unable to engage with is the concept of 'metaphorical truth' (Stephens, 2005: xii): truths which are not derived from 'facts' or 'reality' but which reveal themselves through imaginative works of fiction, including novels and plays. As Siobhan points out to him, 'people like stories, Christopher. Some people find things which are kind of true in things which are made up' (82). *Curious Incident* is a work of fiction which itself reflects on the power of stories, of 'things which are made up', to reveal truths about human experience. Insights into human nature, behaviour, belief and desire enable us to interact socially, and this is precisely the knowledge that Christopher lacks. In this way, the play celebrates the role of the imagination in understanding the realities of the world in which we live.

Things to do

1 Alone or in pairs, reflect on what you have learned about human experience from reading *The Curious Incident of the Dog in the Night-Time*? What do you know or understand now that you didn't before?

2 Stephens provides five examples of phrases that are metaphorical:

   – I am going to seriously lose my rag.
   – He was the apple of her eye.

- They had a skeleton in the closet.
- We had a real pig of a day.
- The dog was stone dead.

- What does each of these metaphors mean?
- In what ways do they foreshadow events later in the narrative?

3 Metaphorical language is typically very specific to its culture. Share some phrases and sayings from different languages. Translate the phrase into English and see if people can guess the meaning before it is explained.

Logic and maths

Christopher derives solace from logic and maths. At times of anxiety, he withdraws into his own world of numbers – doubling twos or counting the cubes of cardinal numbers[3] – in order to comfort, reassure and calm himself down. He likes the order and control of patterned sequences and likes maths because the results of equations are predictable and repeatable. It is not only maths that provides this sense of comfort, however: very important to Christopher is the train set his parents bought him for Christmas two years ago. When faced with an issue that is too complex for him to process, as when he discovers his mother's letters, Christopher busies himself with the repetitive action of assembling the tracks. Assistant director on the original production, Katy Rudd, explains:

> The train track is something that Christopher has both at home and at school and feels really safe with. It's very

---

[3] Cardinal numbers are numbers that say how much of something there are, such as one, two, three, four, five, etc.

methodical, it's very ordered and it's also, of course, something that his mum gave him. Christopher plays with his train set when he's trying to escape something, or when he's trying to work something out. It's like a focusing activity that Christopher can do, while also being a metaphor for him trying to get closer to his mum: literally building the track that will take him to London. (2015)

Christopher loves working out puzzles via deductive logic and reason and his imagination is fired by the real-life mystery of Who Killed Wellington? He is a fan of Sherlock Holmes stories (Siobhan makes reference to this at the beginning of Part Two) and, indeed, *The Curious Incident of the Dog in the Night-Time* takes its title from a short story featuring the famous fictional detective.[4] This reminds us that *Curious Incident* is, at least initially, a murder mystery story: a work of 'whodunit?' detective fiction in which Christopher embarks upon a Holmes-style investigation to uncover the truth of Wellington's death. In the process, however, he uncovers some uncomfortable truths about his life, his family 'and the way adults lie to children and to each other' (Gardner, 2013).

Secrets and lies

When I started writing my book there was only one mystery to solve. Now there were two. (70)

The plot of *The Curious Incident of the Dog in the Night-Time* is structured around two secrets. The first secret is created by the

---

[4] The short story in question is 'Silver Blaze', collected in *The Memoirs of Sherlock Holmes* by Sir Arthur Conan Doyle, first published in 1892.

Inspector Gregory: Is there any other point to which you would wish to draw my attention?
Holmes: To the curious incident of the dog in the night-time.
Inspector Gregory: The dog did nothing in the night-time.
Holmes: That was the curious incident.

lie Ed tells Christopher about the death of his mother, Judy. The second secret is created by the truth Ed hides from Christopher about the killing of Mrs Shears's dog, Wellington. Each of these major secrets contains a smaller secret within them: firstly, that Judy had an affair with Mr Shears and, secondly, that Ed began a relationship with Mrs Shears which ended acrimoniously.

The centrality of secrets to the plot of *Curious Incident* sits in ironic contrast to the protagonist's inability to tell lies. 'I do not tell lies', Christopher tells us. 'Mother used to say that this was because I was a good person. But it is not because I am a good person. It is because I can't tell lies' (32). Before the discovery of his mother's letters, it is important to Christopher that people know he 'always tells the truth', and this phrase, or variations of it, occur in his conversations with a Duty Sergeant (38), Mrs Alexander (57) and Siobhan (62). He is, as critic Laura Thompson observed, 'a remorseless truth-teller', a characteristic that 'becomes particularly forceful' when compared with 'the fuzzy morality of "normal" people' (2012).

Interestingly, however, as the play progresses Christopher becomes aware that there is a distinction between 'telling the truth' and 'being honest' and that you can be truthful without necessarily being honest. When Christopher returns home from talking with Mrs Alexander about Mr Shears (whose name Ed has expressly forbidden Christopher to mention), Christopher is able to modify his response so that, while not directly lying, he does not necessarily tell the whole truth.

Ed   And what have you been up to, young man?

Christopher   I went to the shop to get some liquorice laces and a Milky Bar.

Ed   You were a long time.

Christopher   I talked to Mrs Alexander's dog outside the shop.[5] (61)

---

[5] Mrs Alexander confirms she has a dog on p. 51.

Similarly, when Christopher reads the first letter from his mother his father distractedly asks him what he is doing. Christopher replies 'I'm reading a letter' but, unusually for him, does not disclose any further information (70). It is a guarded truth, suggesting that Christopher is developing an independence of mind which frees him from the reflex to tell the truth (a reflex that has, at times, left him vulnerable, as when he admits to hitting the policeman on purpose).

Where Christopher's guarded truths are designed to protect him from his father's temper, the lies Ed tells are designed to protect Christopher from the hurt that knowing the truth would cause. This strategy, however, fails spectacularly when Christopher discovers his mother's letters, causing him a great deal of pain and confusion. In a desperate attempt to salvage their relationship, Ed acknowledges his failure and seeks, albeit too late, to rectify his mistakes:

> **Ed**   Life is difficult, you know. It's bloody hard telling the truth all the time. But I want you to know that I'm trying [. . .] You have to know that I am going to tell you the truth from now on. About everything. Because . . . if you don't tell the truth now, then later on it hurts even more. (78–79)

Interestingly, Ed's way of caring for Christopher stands in stark contrast to that of Siobhan's. Siobhan never lies to Christopher, even if the truth is sometimes unwanted, uncomfortable or troubling to Christopher. Indeed, Siobhan's refusal to mislead or lie to Christopher generates the crackling tension in the play's final moments, as she remains silent in the face of Christopher's repeated questioning:

> **Christopher**   Does that mean I can do anything, do you think?
>
> Does that mean I can do anything, Siobhan?
>
> Does that mean I can do anything? (130)

'It's an agonizing question for her', observes Stephens. 'She can't answer it because it would be a lie to answer it positively and it would be a brutal gesture to answer it negatively' (2015). Siobhan is clear-sighted about Christopher's long-term prospects, and she would rather be honest than offer him the cheap comfort of false hope.

Fallibility of adults and adult relationships

To be fallible is to be capable of making mistakes. It is a trait shared by everyone – indeed, it is what makes us human. Growing up, however, it can often come as a surprise to learn that adults, our parents or guardians in particular, are *not* *in*fallible: that despite their advanced years(!) and experience, they too can make mistakes, behave badly and fail in their relationships. *Curious Incident* offers a compassionate portrayal of the struggles and mistakes of Judy and Ed with Christopher (see also 'Character') but the fallibility of adults is a theme which recurs throughout the whole play. There are, in total, four relationships which break down within the story: Mrs Shears and Mr Shears, who divorce because of Roger's affair with Judy; Ed and Judy, who separate in part because of Judy's affair; Ed and Mrs Shears, whose friendship is compromised by Ed's assumption that Mrs Shears will, in some sense, replace Judy; and Judy and Mr Shears, who we only ever see arguing.

With significant exceptions, such as Siobhan and Mrs Alexander, the play's adults repeatedly fail to demonstrate the kindness, responsibility and restraint with which we might expect grown men and women to treat Christopher. Policemen swear at him ('If you try any of that monkey-business again, you little shit, I am going to seriously lose my rag' [34]) and react in disgust to his distress ('Oh Christ, you've wet yourself. For God's sake, go to the bloody toilet, will you?' [94]). Train passengers are too busy or drunk to worry about why a teenage boy might be hiding in a luggage rack (95), and shopkeepers insult and patronize him ('Is that the A–Z?/No, it's a sodding crocodile' [105]). Roger Shears gets drunk and threatens Christopher – 'You think you're so bloody clever, don't you?' (119) – and Mrs Shears taunts Judy in front of Christopher: 'So has he finally dumped you too? [. . .] You had it coming. Don't try and pretend that you didn't. Because you bloody did' (122). *Curious Incident*'s unsentimental look at the way that adults can treat teenagers, and each other, dispels the myth that grown-ups are always in possession of all the answers. Even Reverend Peters, an otherwise benevolent figure in the play, makes an excuse and leaves when he is unable to answer Christopher's questions about God: 'Christopher, we should talk about this on another day when I have more time' (45).

While the emotional complexity of adults – their insecurities, motivations and desires – may be entirely indecipherable to Christopher, *Curious Incident* suggests that this complexity in fact poses a challenge to us all. As Ed remarks of Mrs Shears, 'I think she cared more for that bloody dog than for us. And maybe that's not so stupid looking back. Maybe it's easier living on your own looking after some stupid mutt than sharing your life with other actual human beings' (79).

Family

The family drama at the heart of *Curious Incident* asks interesting questions about the resilience of familial bonds, the place of 'home', and the functioning of a nuclear family (a family unit in which two married parents and their children live in the same residence).

From Judy's letters we can infer that for most of Christopher's upbringing she was his primary caregiver. When her toes were broken, however, meaning she 'couldn't walk properly for a month' (76), his father stepped into this role. Seeing how well Christopher responded to his dad, Judy convinced herself that they were better off without her. It is interesting that, for Judy, leaving the family home does not mean severing all ties with Christopher: she writes to him because she hopes they can continue to have a relationship. It is Ed who decides that by leaving home Judy forfeits the right to have any contact with Christopher and, henceforth, he takes full responsibility for Christopher's welfare.

When Ed confesses to killing Wellington, however, Christopher's home transforms overnight from a place of safety into place of danger. Christopher carefully distinguishes between the categories of 'family', 'friend' and 'stranger' and knows that to be safe he must go to either a friend or family member. In Christopher's eyes, Siobhan is neither friend nor family because she is a teacher. Uncle Terry is family member but he smokes and strokes Christopher's hair, so he is not really a friend. Mrs Alexander tells Christopher that she is a friend, but he is adamant that she is 'a stranger' (60). It is his mother that Christopher goes to, despite the hazards of travelling to London by himself. Even with no idea of where the journey to find his mother will lead him, Christopher's rejection of his family home is absolute: 'Swindon's not my home any more' he tells his father. 'My home is 451c Chapter Road, London NW2 5NG' (102).

When Judy and Christopher return to Swindon together, Christopher refuses any contact with his dad. We learn from a conversation with Siobhan that when Christopher is forced to spend time at his house he 'push[es] the bed up against the door in case Father tries to come in':

Sometimes he tries to talk to me through the door. I don't answer him. Sometimes he sits outside the door quietly for a long time. (127)

Christopher's rejection leaves Ed distraught. One day, Ed sets a kitchen timer and asks for just five minutes of his son's time:

Christopher, look . . . Things can't go on like this. I don't know about you, but this . . . this just hurts too much. You being in the house but refusing to talk to me. You have to

learn to trust me . . . And I don't care how long it takes . . .
if [. . .] it takes years I don't care. Because this is important.
This is more important than anything else. (128)

Ed's gift of the puppy is an apology for his actions, a way of
asking Christopher to spend time with him, and a means of
proving to his son that he can be trusted. The Boone's family
story ends on a note of reconciliation and hope: Judy has
returned; Christopher is rebuilding a relationship with his dad
and, although they remain separated, Ed and Judy also seem to
be working towards some kind of restored partnership. As
Nicola Walker observes, by the end of the play 'they work as
an unusual family unit and, you know, that's better than not
having a unit at all' (2015).

Things to do

Look over the main themes discussed in this section and
select any that also relate to the Shakespeare play that
you have studied. Choose one theme that the plays have in
common and compare how Stephens and Shakespeare have
chosen to dramatize it.

Character

Curious Incident features a colossal cast of forty-one characters!
These range from named individuals such as Christopher,
Siobhan, Ed and Judy, to generic characters such as 'Policeman
One' and 'Station Guard', to even more elusive figures such as
'Woman on Heath' and the intriguing 'Man with Socks'. Many
of these characters appear for no more than a couple of lines
because their function within the play is to move the story
forward and we do not need to know them in great detail for

this to happen. You are not expected to remember every single character in the play but it is worth remembering that, in addition to the main roles, *Curious Incident* features a large supporting cast played by an ensemble of actors, each one of whom is likely to multi-role up to half a dozen of these smaller parts.

This section will focus on the main named characters in the play-text. As well as understanding what each character is like you will also need to develop an appreciation of *how Stephens constructs each character*. While it may be tempting to think and talk about these characters as though they are real people, they are in fact fictions, crafted by the playwright to create a certain effect. When a character does something that makes us laugh, or feel upset, or become thoughtful, try to ask yourself *how* has the playwright created that moment? What is it about the language, or the timing, or the images onstage that has created that desired effect?

Christopher

Christopher is a fifteen-year-old-boy with behavioural difficulties who lives with his father, Ed, in Swindon. He has been told by his dad that his mother is dead but, while investigating the murder of a neighbour's dog, Christopher discovers that his mother is in fact alive and living in London. Their reunion results in Judy returning to Swindon, where she and Christopher live together while he and his father rebuild their relationship.

As previously discussed, Christopher's behaviour and abilities correspond to various traits commonly associated with autism. He screams and lashes out if he is touched; replies to questions with excessively detailed answers ('I'm fifteen years and three months and two days' [33]); and cannot be parted from his watch because of an obsessive need to 'know exactly what time it is' (35). When asked about his family, Christopher replies that his family is 'Father and Mother but

Mother's dead' (36). The dispassion with which Christopher states that his mother is dead – contrasted with the anxiety he experiences at the thought of losing his watch – suggests that Christopher's ability to form emotional attachments with people is underdeveloped or impaired in some way.

We learn about Christopher both from what he says and does *and* from what he has written about himself in his book. We learn that his full name is Christopher John Francis Boone and that he knows the capital city of every country and every prime number up to 7507. He has exceptional facilities of memory, together with an impressive aptitude for maths and a fascination with outer space. He likes small spaces so long as there is no one else in there with him and likes to sit in the airing cupboard 'and think for hours' (53). He may display an emotional disconnect from his immediate surroundings but – as when he explains the Milky Way to his dad in the police station (36–37), or leaps into a fantasy about becoming an astronaut (53–54) – it is clear that Christopher's mind is alert, inquisitive and incredibly agile.

Things to do

Read the list of items that are found in Christopher's pockets on p. 35.

- What 'clues' to his personality does this list provide you with? Consider both the items themselves and the way they are described.

Statistics, facts and logic are reassuring to Christopher, in contrast to social interaction with other people, which he finds very difficult. People are 'confusing' to Christopher, firstly because he finds it difficult to interpret facial expressions and, secondly, because people 'often talk using metaphors' – that is, using words or phrases that mean one thing to mean or suggest something else (39). Christopher's computer-like mind struggles to comprehend 'information' that requires *interpretation*, or the use of *social imagination*, in order to understand what someone means – as when someone raises an eyebrow to indicate they are unimpressed, or uses figurative language for colour and emphasis: 'it was a real pig of a day'. His literal-mindedness also means that he 'can't tell lies' (32) as he is unable, for example, to pretend that something happened when it didn't. This is why Christopher dislikes metaphors and acting: 'because it is pretending that something is real when it is not really real at all so it is like a kind of lie' (82).

While in some respects we might commend Christopher's commitment to what he would regard as 'the facts' or 'reality' or 'the truth' of things, his inability to imagine himself in someone else's shoes (to 'pretend' for a moment that he is not him but someone else) also means that he is severely limited in his ability to understand the intentions, needs and feelings of other people – even of those closest to him. When Ed makes a heartfelt apology to Christopher after their fight, for instance, Christopher accepts his father's offer to touch fingertips. It appears to be a tender moment of forgiveness and reconciliation between father and son but, for Christopher, this is not a moment of emotional contact: his thoughts are not with his father, or with the recent fight, but with where Ed has put his book: 'Is it in the dustbin at the front of the house?' (65). Similarly, when Judy finds out that Christopher thought she was dead, Christopher does not understand why she begins to 'howl' with grief and anger. When she asks Christopher if she might 'just for once' hold his hand, he is unable to recognize the emotional significance of this and refuses: 'I don't like people holding my hand' (109).

While Christopher may struggle to understand social interaction and the complexity of human relationships, he is not innately aggressive or cruel, as his ability to care for his pet rat Toby – and to care about what happened to Wellington – demonstrate. While Christopher finds it difficult to empathize with the emotions that cause other people to behave in certain ways, we also see him struggle to interpret and process his own emotional responses. The discovery of his mother's letters, for example, initially presents nothing more than a second 'mystery to solve' and a sharpening of his detective skills: 'I decided that I would not think about it any more that night because I didn't have enough information and could easily LEAP TO THE WRONG CONCLUSIONS' (70). When he reads the remaining letters the next day, however, the shock of realizing that his mother is alive induces a severe seizure: he thrashes, '*hitting his hands and his feet and his head against the floor*', until he is sick (75). When Ed confesses that it was he who killed Wellington, it is apparently this revelation – not the truth about his mother – that prompts Christopher to panic and run away: 'Father had murdered Wellington. That meant he could murder me. I had to get out of the house' (80). When he reaches his mum's house, he explains to her that 'I'm going to live with you because father killed Wellington with a garden fork and I'm frightened of him' (107). Only later, when Judy asks him why he didn't write, does Christopher tell her that his father told him she was dead. Christopher's fixation with Wellington's fate, as with his later fixation on sitting his A-Level Maths exam, dominates Christopher's mental landscape. Both obsessions seem to cause him as much, if not more, emotional and physical distress as learning the truth of his parents' recent history.

While Christopher's emotions remain turbulent throughout the course of the play (the prospect of his A-Level Maths exam being postponed prompts him to throw a tantrum and stop eating or sleeping properly), there are also indications of a developing confidence. The clearest example of this is the courage he shows in venturing beyond his familiar surroundings to find his mum in London. In the words of actor Luke Treadaway, going from Swindon to London is, for Christopher, 'like you or I going to the moon' (2015). The journey exposes Christopher to encounters and situations which, because new and unfamiliar to him, are fraught with risk and danger. Travelling to London forces him to talk to strangers, confront the chaos of train stations, negotiate the tube and navigate the streets of London; for Christopher these situations represent significant personal challenges which he must overcome if he is to reach his mother's flat. That he successfully finds his way to Willesden is a testament to Christopher's determination and strength, qualities that perhaps he didn't know he even possessed.

From being immersed entirely in his own world, Christopher begins to develop an awareness of his own difference, as he starts to realize that the logic and rules that govern his beliefs and behaviour are at odds with the logic and rules that govern the beliefs and behaviour of the adults around him. For example, in Christopher's world, killing a dog is a very terrible crime, so when Judy explains that his father will only be arrested for killing Wellington if Mrs Shears presses charges, Christopher is confused. 'Is killing Wellington a little crime?' he asks, to be told by his mother that 'yes love it is' (121). Similarly, when towards the end of the play Siobhan tells Christopher that he cannot come to live with her, he asks if it is 'because I'm too noisy and sometimes I'm "difficult to control"' (127). Learning that his view of the world isn't a view shared by everyone is an important realization for Christopher, and reconciling this contradiction is an important step on his journey towards greater self-awareness. It is, arguably, this emergent self-knowledge that enables him to tolerate living in a place where 'the corridor's painted brown' and 'other people use the toilet' (126) even though it causes him distress ('sometimes other people are in there so I do wet myself' [126]). Most importantly, by the end of the play Christopher is willing to spend time alone with his father, as Ed works to re-establish a relationship with his son.

Christopher ends the play with a new-found confidence which leads him to declare that he is going to go university, get a First-Class Honours degree and become a scientist. Whether or not we believe that he will indeed go on to achieve these aims, this final scene presents us with a glimpse of Christopher's far-reaching ambition; a potential realized in the play's 'postscript' where, with vibrant theatrical flair, Christopher solves a maths problem in front of the audience.

Things to do

In 'Behind the Scenes', actor Luke Treadaway describes an exercise that he did in preparation for playing the role of Christopher. Try this exercise for yourself: read the script (or a particular section of script) and write down:

(a) A list of facts about Christopher. For example:

He likes the colour red and 'metal colour' (58).

He likes being alone in small spaces.

He likes looking at the rain.

(b) A list of what other people say about Christopher. For example:

He's a 'bloody handful'.

(c) A list of what Christopher says about other people. For example:

Uncle Terry smokes cigarettes and strokes Christopher's hair.

Read over your lists. What do they reveal about Christopher's character? What questions about him are you left with?

Ed

Ed Boone separated from Christopher's mother two years ago. In a misguided attempt to protect his son from the knowledge that his mother left them, he told Christopher that she died from a heart attack. When Christopher discovers that this is a lie, Ed decides that he must tell Christopher the whole truth. He confesses to killing Wellington, which prompts Christopher to run away; when Christopher returns to Swindon with his mother, Ed begins the painful process of regaining the trust of his son.

Ed presents a complex character study. While he has many flaws, these should be weighed against both the challenges of caring for a child whose needs are as difficult as Christopher's and the love which – although at times clumsily expressed – Ed clearly feels for his teenage son. Ed can be rough and aggressive but he is also capable of tenderness, gentleness and remorse.

Interestingly, an important clue to understanding the character of Ed – to understanding what motivates him to make certain choices and take certain actions – is provided not by Ed himself but by Judy, in one of the letters she writes to Christopher: 'I'm not like your father', she writes, 'Your father is a much more patient person. He just gets on with things and if things upset him he doesn't let it show' (74). From this description, we can begin to think about Ed as someone who bottles up his feelings – who 'just gets on with things', no matter how hurt or sad or worried he may be. When the play opens, Ed has had a tough two years: his wife has left him, his subsequent relationship with Mrs Shears ended badly and he has been raising single-handedly a child with social and behavioural problems. Indeed, the first time we see Ed, he is picking up Christopher from the police station; his repeated requests for Christopher to 'stay out of trouble' suggest not only the frequency with which Christopher gets into trouble but also the strain that this places on Ed. As he later says in anger to Judy:

> I cooked his meals. I cleaned his clothes. I looked after
> him every weekend. I looked after him when he was ill. I
> took him to the doctor. I worried myself sick every time he
> wandered off somewhere at night. I went to school every
> time he got into a fight. (111)

Just as Christopher struggles to interpret and process his feelings, Ed finds it difficult to articulate and express his emotions, preferring instead that they be ignored or buried. When Ed attacks Wellington with a garden fork it is an uncontrolled expression of anger and frustration: 'Maybe if I'd just given it a kick it would probably have backed off', he admits in retrospect. 'But, shit Christopher, when the red mist comes down ... [it] was like everything I'd been bottling up for two years just ...' (79). Christopher's determination to find Wellington's killer places an extra strain on an already pressured situation. Ed's fears that Christopher might discover the truth about his mother, combined with his frustration at Christopher's un-cooperative behaviour, find expression in a series of increasingly angry exchanges. These outbursts culminate in a physical fight where Ed deliberately grabs hold of Christopher and shakes him. Christopher responds by punching Ed 'repeatedly in the face' (64), which prompts Ed to knock Christopher to the ground.

Ed's regret at hitting his son is immediate and heartfelt. Often when Ed speaks he lacks confidence, stutters and has trouble finishing sentences. Apologizing after their fight, however, he is at his most eloquent:

> I'm sorry I hit you. I didn't mean to. I love you very much, Christopher. Don't ever forget that. I know I lose my rag occasionally. And I know I shouldn't. But I only do it because I worry about you, because I don't want to see you getting into trouble, because I don't want you to get hurt. Do you understand? (65)

Ed and Christopher's fight reveals both Ed's exasperation with Christopher and the lengths to which he is prepared to go in order to prevent him from 'getting hurt'. It also reveals, however, the extent to which Ed is trapped by his own lies. While designed to protect Christopher, these lies – about Judy, about Mrs Shears and now about Wellington – are beginning to damage Ed's relationship with Christopher. When Christopher discovers his mother's letters, Ed can offer no explanation: 'I don't know what to say ... I was in such a mess ... It got out of control' (77). He realizes, however, that their relationship threatens to collapse entirely, and makes a desperate attempt to repair it: 'You have to know that I am going to tell you the truth from now on. About everything' (78–79). This moment is a turning-point for Ed as, for the first time, he faces the consequences of the ill-judged decisions he made in moments of crisis.

Ed has his flaws and weaknesses but his devotion to Christopher is consistent and can be observed in seemingly mundane daily activities: he prepares Christopher's often eccentric choice of meals; he looks out for programmes that Christopher will like; asks after his day at school and is reluctant to leave Christopher on his own in the house. Even when Christopher runs away, Ed's anger and fear swiftly transform into concern and support as he 'guides' Christopher onto the tube train: 'It'll really scare you [. . .] Try not to let it [. . .] Figure it out. Get the rhythm right' (102). Ed is neither as articulate nor as academically gifted as his son – Christopher's elegant soliloquies about astronomy and science are typically met with either monosyllabic responses or a plea for him to 'give it a bit of a break, mate' (54) – but he recognizes and appreciates Christopher's prodigious mathematical gifts and insists, despite Mrs Gascoyne's protests, that Christopher take his Maths A-Level. Few of Ed's efforts are acknowledged or reciprocated by Christopher, who shares no interests with his father, prefers to be by himself and will not be touched, let alone hugged. Ed's love, however, is unconditional. He is devastated by Christopher's rejection and determines to regain his son's trust, however difficult the process may be: 'I don't care how long it takes . . . Because this is important. This is more important than anything else' (128). The tentative reconciliation between father and son at the play's close – the gift of the puppy, the gardening, the plans for a Further Maths A-Level the following year – testifies to Ed's perseverance and unwavering commitment to his son.

Things to do

1 Read the following sections:

- pp. 39–40 *from* '**Christopher:** I'm sorry' *to* '**Ed:** You could very well say that'.

- pp. 52–53 *from* '**Ed:** Where have you been?' *to* '**Ed:** And you know what it means when I make you promise'.

- pp. 63–65 *from* '**Ed:** What is this?' *to* '**Ed:** I need a drink'.

In pairs, discuss:

- What is Ed angry about?

- Who is Ed angry at?

- What is he afraid of?

2 Imagine a conversation between Ed and Rhodri the day after Ed and Christopher fight. Rhodri is curious to know how Ed has received his bruises. Write this conversation in the form of a dialogue between the two characters, like a script.

Judy

Judy Boone is Christopher's mother. She left Ed and Christopher to live with Roger Shears in London two years ago. Unbeknown to Christopher, she has regularly written to him throughout this period, despite not receiving any reply. When Christopher arrives on her doorstep, she immediately takes him in and looks after him. While initially furious at Ed for the lie he told, Judy tolerates and eventually assists in his attempts to rebuild a relationship with Christopher.

Judy is introduced to us through Christopher's memories and her letters. We first glimpse her when Christopher remembers a family holiday in Cornwall. She is on the beach at Polperro, sunbathing, swimming and encouraging Christopher to paddle in the sea. She dives under the water but Christopher screams, so she wades back to the shore to touch fingers and coax him to be quiet. In the same memory, Judy playfully fantasizes about life with a lover in the South of France. While only said in jest, this small act of escapism hints at the longing for different circumstances that Judy will later act upon. Indeed, the next time we encounter Judy, she has moved to London with Mr Shears and Christopher is discovering the letters she has written to him. While only three of these letters are read out, they reveal much about Judy's character, including her temperament, her relationship with Ed and the love she feels for her son.

Judy describes herself as 'not a very good mother' to Christopher, explaining how she lacked the patience to cope with his condition (74). She provides a candid account of how difficult it was to deal with his behaviour, reminding Christopher of the time in Bentall's when 'you just lay on the floor and screamed and banged your hands and feet on the floor' (74). She describes how that night she 'just cried and cried and cried' (ibid). When she told Ed that she 'couldn't take it any more', he got 'really cross and told me I was being stupid' so she hit him (ibid.). Unable to cope with Christopher's tantrums, Judy's doubts about her ability to take care of him led to further arguments with Ed. 'By the end we stopped talking to each other very much', she writes, 'And I felt really lonely' (ibid.). Judy began an affair with Mr Shears but was not willing to leave Christopher. After an incident where her toes were broken by Christopher throwing a chopping board, however, Ed had to take over his care while she recovered. 'I remember looking at the two of you' she writes, 'and thinking how you were really different with him. Much calmer. And it made me so sad because it was like you didn't need me at all' (76).

Having persuaded herself that to leave would be 'the best for all of us' (76), Judy, like Ed, is trapped by her own decision.

That she misses her son very much is evident from not only the number of letters she writes – forty-three over two years – but also from the details she includes. She is pleased, for example, to tell him that she now works as a secretary for a factory 'that makes things out of steel. You'd like it a lot' (69) and describes how happy remembering Christopher playing with his train set makes her. She asks whether he has solved the puzzle she sent him as a present, wonders whether he still wants to be an astronaut and hopes that he is 'still doing maths' (77). Significantly, and in contrast to Ed, Judy attempts to tell Christopher the truth of what happened: 'I know you might not understand any of this but I wanted to try to explain so that you knew' (75).

Judy is overjoyed when Christopher turns up on her doorstep and takes him in immediately without question. Once reunited with Christopher, Judy is headstrong in her determination to keep him with her: she has a stand-up argument with Ed, who she tries to prevent from seeing Christopher, and dictates to a peeved Roger that Christopher will be staying with them indefinitely. When Roger's behaviour turns threatening, Judy leaves immediately: 'someone was going to get hurt', she tells Christopher, 'And I don't necessarily mean you' (120). The single-mindedness she demonstrated when she left her family is directed towards establishing a new life for her and Christopher. She returns to Swindon, finding herself a new job and accommodation for her and Christopher.

Judy, like Ed, has her flaws. Her letters reveal not only an acknowledged lack of patience, but also a tendency towards self-pity and reluctance to accept her responsibilities. She can, in her own way, be as obstinate as Christopher and she is still learning how to reconcile the conflict between her own and Christopher's needs. Spending two years apart from Christopher, however, has revealed to her just how much she loves and needs her son. When given a second chance to be a mother to Christopher, Judy seizes the opportunity and determines this time to persevere.

Things to Do

In 'Behind the Scenes', Nicola Walker talks of thinking about 'what went unspoken in Judy's letters, what's really underneath some of that positivity and attempt to reach out to her son' (Walker, 2015).

- Read the following sections:

  pp. 69–70: *from* '**Judy**: 451c Chapter Road, Willesdon, London NW2 5NG' *to* 'Lots of love, Your Mum'.

  p. 73: *from* '**Judy**: 451c Chapter Road, Willesdon, London NW2 5NG' to 'I liked remembering that a lot'.

- What do you think might be 'unspoken' in these letters? Choose one of these letters and re-write it as though Judy were writing to a close friend rather than to her teenage son. You may wish to consider:

Letter one

(a) What Judy thinks about her job at the steel factory.

(b) What Judy thinks of the flat her and Roger have moved into.

(c) How Judy feels about not receiving a reply from Christopher.

Letter two

(a) Why Judy pulled out the photo album and looked through old photos.

(b) How she feels about spending Christmas without Christopher.

(c) What the other 'really good times' that she, Ed and Christopher spent together were.

Siobhan

Siobhan is Christopher's teacher. It is at her suggestion that Christopher writes the book that becomes the play. The character of Siobhan also helps to narrate the action of the play: she reads out loud from Christopher's book and sometimes speaks *as* Christopher, as when he fantasizes about becoming an astronaut or does his 'detecting' around the house (66–68). She also reads out sections of Judy's letters.

The play reveals very little biographical detail about Siobhan, other than the fact that she is twenty-seven years old and a teacher at Christopher's school (31). We do not know where she lives, whether she is married or whether she has children. She exists only in relation to Christopher, for whom she provides a kind of sanctuary: a safe space removed from the messy emotions and tangled lies of his parents. With Siobhan, Christopher plays, learns, thinks, imagines and makes hypotheses as to the identity of Wellington's killer. The most sustained conversations Christopher has are with Siobhan: he confides in her, remembers his mother with her, and sometimes chats to her in his head, as when he goes for a walk in London at night (114–116). In turn, Siobhan offers Christopher support, encouragement, reassurance and inspiration. She is the only character with access into Christopher's mind, and the only character who can speak to Christopher about his maths: 'What's the logarithmic formula for the approximate number of prime numbers not greater than x?' she asks, as she attempts to get his brain working before his A-Level (124). Siobhan often responds to Christopher's chatter with attentive questions which help him focus and develop his train of thought; she never orders Christopher to do (or not do) something and she doesn't put any pressure on him to behave a certain way. Before Christopher sits his A-Level, for example, Siobhan is careful to ensure that this is, in fact, what he wants: 'If you say you don't want to do it no one is going to be angry with you. And it won't be wrong or illegal or stupid. It will just be what you want and that will be fine' (ibid.). Similarly, once she has established that Christopher isn't scared to go home, she accepts that Christopher doesn't want to talk any more about the fight with his dad and lets the matter drop.

Up until Christopher is reunited with Judy, Siobhan is the central female figure in his life. When he is frightened at Swindon train station, it is Siobhan who 'appears' to guide him through the noisy and crowded underpass, encouraging him to imagine 'a big red line' through the tunnel, and to 'count the rhythm' in his head, 'like when you're doing music or drumming. Left, right, left, right . . .' (91). She appears again at Paddington Station and once more when Christopher goes for a walk at night in London. When he sits his exam, it is Siobhan's suggestions for keeping calm that he remembers: 'Stop groaning. Get your breath. Count the cubes of the cardinal numbers again' (125). When Christopher achieves his A grade, Siobhan's uncharacteristic inarticulacy – 'Oh. Oh. That's just. That's terrific, Christopher' (129) – suggests that she is momentarily overwhelmed by the pride she feels for her student.

Siobhan and Christopher share a bond of affection and trust that is unique to them. Siobhan's professional integrity, however, ensures that she does not allow herself to become a substitute or surrogate parent to Christopher. She consistently advises Christopher that he should do what his father tells him to and, importantly, she hands over Christopher's book when Ed 'goes to Siobhan' and 'reaches his hand out for it' (62). As Stephens observes, while Siobhan would want to protect Christopher from the consequences of Ed reading the book, 'she would have to defer to Ed. She is, importantly, *not* Christopher's parent. Teachers can't replace parents' (quoted in Bunyan and Moore, 2013: 128).[6] This point is reinforced with some poignancy when, towards the end of the play, Christopher asks Siobhan whether he might come and live with her:

---

[6] Interestingly, Stephens also notes that 'in the original production at the National the director Marianne Elliott chose not to have Ed take the book from Siobhan but rather just to find it. Clearly she agreed with the teacher! (quoted in Bunyan and Moore, 2013: 128).

Siobhan　No, Christopher, you can't.

Christopher　Why can't I? Is it because I'm too noisy and sometimes I'm 'difficult to control'?

Siobhan　No, it's because I'm not your mother, Christopher.

Christopher　No.

Siobhan　That's very important, Christopher. Do you understand that?

Christopher　I don't know. (127)

Niamh Cusack, who played Siobhan in the original National Theatre production, suggests that:

> when Siobhan says 'I'm not your mother', it is as much for herself as for Christopher. I think it's a reminder. There are times when a teacher has to take a deep breath and step back and I think there are times in this play when Siobhan comes dangerously close to simply loving this boy. To remain the good teacher, which she is, she must step back. She must have objectivity, which is something I observed in the teachers I shadowed at the schools I visited. (2015)

Mrs Alexander

Mrs Alexander is an elderly lady who lives in Christopher's street. She is a little deaf and has a grandson Christopher's age. Unlike most of the other adults Christopher encounters, she does not make fun of or patronize Christopher but instead seeks to engage him in friendly conversation, asking him about his interests and hobbies. It is Mrs Alexander who reveals to Christopher that his mother had an affair with Mr Shears.

Mrs Shears

Mrs Shears is Christopher's neighbour. She is the owner of Wellington, the dead dog whose discovery starts the play. She is divorced from her husband, Mr Shears, with whom Judy had an affair. After Judy left, she and Ed began a relationship but this deteriorated into a series of rows which resulted, one night, in Ed attacking her dog.

Mr Shears (Roger)

Mr Shears was married to Mrs Shears when he began an affair with Judy. We first meet him in the middle of an argument with Judy, after he has said something to embarrass or upset her. He undermines Judy's efforts to care for Christopher and his threatening behaviour convinces her to leave him and return to Swindon with Christopher.

Dramatic technique

Structure

Plays are typically divided into two or more *acts* which are composed of a number of discrete *scenes*. *Curious Incident* is unusual in that it is simply arranged into two Parts, without further formal scene division. Once the play has begun, the action onstage is continuous and does not stop until the end of Part One, where the interval falls; similarly, once Part Two is underway the stage is in constant motion until the lights fall on Siobhan and Christopher. At this point, however, the play is not quite finished. After the curtain call, Christopher returns with a treat for the audience: the 'Postscript', or 'Maths Appendix', where he demonstrates how he solved his favourite A-Level Maths question. Christopher's demonstration is a *coup de theatre* – a surprise theatrical gesture staged for maximum dramatic impact – which ends the story of *Curious Incident* on a joyous, celebratory note of achievement: 'when [Christopher] returns after the curtain call to expound further on [his] numerate gifts', noted one reviewer, 'the realm of mathematics seems newly miraculous' (Wolf, 2012).

An important point to note about the play's structure is that the events of Part One are not presented in chronological order. The arrangement of time is not linear; instead, the story jumps backwards and forwards between Christopher's discovery of Wellington and his decision to write a book about it. There are flashback scenes between Ed and Christopher, and a 'memory' scene in which Christopher remembers his mother. As assistant director Katy Rudd explains:

> This is Christopher's book, his story, and Simon reflects this in his chronology. The play jump-cuts to bits of the story that Christopher finds most interesting; we move, as if in Christopher's brain, to what's important. (2015)

There are, moreover, moments when the narrative seems momentarily suspended, as when Christopher imagines being an astronaut or explains why he finds people confusing. These moments might seem like unnecessary or confusing digressions from the main narrative but in fact they provide us with insights into Christopher's mind, and reveal to us something of how he perceives the world. Part Two is slightly more straightforward: after the opening scene introduces the framing device of a play within a play (see below), Christopher's personal odyssey to London and all further narrative events are presented in the chronological order in which they occur.

Things to Do

1 In pairs or small groups, discuss:

   - Why does Stephens chose to omit formal scene divisions in favour of a continuous stream of action?
   - What effect does this have on an audience?

2 In order to help the cast and creative team navigate their way through Stephens's script, director Marianne Elliott introduced scene numbers and names for each episode.

- As a class or individually, go through Stephens's script and insert Act and Scene numbers before each episode. For example: Act I, sc. i would be

    From – p. 31: *A dead dog lies in the middle of the stage*

    To – p. 34: *Policeman One*: . . . Is that understood?

    Act I, sc. ii would be

    From – p. 34: **Siobhan**: I find people confusing

    To – p. 34: **Siobhan**: And it can also mean 'I think that what you just said was very stupid'.

    And so on.

- Once you have inserted Act and Scene numbers, go back over these episodes and try to give each one a name, such as 'School' or 'Home'. Be careful – this might be trickier for some episodes than for others! Carrying out this exercise will provide you with a 'map' of the play which should be helpful for your revision.

Central to the play's mixture of narrated and enacted action is the role of the ensemble: in the original National Theatre production, ten actors played forty-one speaking parts between them. It was important to director Marianne Elliott that the audience were entirely 'immersed' in the action, 'breathing the same air as Christopher, completely inside his head' (National Theatre Discover, 2012). To achieve this, the auditorium was configured 'in-the-round', so that the audience sat all around the playing space. When not required in a scene, the actors sat on white boxes placed around the edges and watched Christopher, 'focusing on whatever he focuses on and all the time giving energy into the centre of the space' (Rudd, 2015). As Elliott explains:

Everything is to do with Christopher, everything is to do with his brain and how he works things out. So if he decides that he wants to be in the kitchen for two lines,

he's in the kitchen for two lines and up has to jump his
father [from the side of the stage]. If he decides he wants
to be in Polperro, he's in Polperro, for ten lines and his
mother has to come up. The ensemble support whatever
Christopher wants in order to tell the story. They have to
follow him and be there with him. (2015)

The use of an ensemble of actors to multi-role a variety of
characters encourages an appreciation of the skill and
technique involved in performing a play, producing a
heightened sense of theatricality particularly apt for a play
which is partly about the act of putting on a play. That *Curious
Incident* is a play within a play is only revealed in Part Two,
when it emerges that Christopher's school has turned his book
into a play for 'everybody' to 'join in [with] and play a part in'
(82). In the words of Simon Stephens, the decision to use the
framing device of a play within a play:

> comes out of the spirit and the sense that Mark Haddon's
> novel is a novel about writing a novel. So if the novel's a
> novel about writing a novel, I wanted the play to be a play
> about making a play! I think these little reminders that
> you're watching a play [such as when Christopher stops the
> action to redirect the actors onstage, or tells an actor he is
> 'too old' to play a part] welcome you into the theatre and
> welcome you into an art form that's completely unique.
> I wanted to celebrate the essence of theatricality because
> I love the theatre. I think it's our best art form. (2015)

Language

There is an interesting layering of 'texts' in *Curious Incident*,
with several different sources informing the play-script. Firstly,
there is Mark Haddon's book itself, as much of the main
characters' dialogue is lifted directly from the original novel
(see Stephens in 'Behind the Scenes'). Secondly, and in keeping
with the novel, there is a nod to the genre of detective fiction, as

evidenced by the delight that Christopher takes in using phrases such as 'Prime Suspect', 'Double Bluff', 'At Large' and 'LEAP TO THE WRONG CONCLUSIONS'. Thirdly (also from the novel), Christopher's experiences in Swindon and Paddington trains stations are written simply as lists of station notices, signs, brand names, and newspaper headlines – what we might call 'found texts' which exist outside the fiction and are taken and arranged into a kind of dramatic collage. Fourthly, there is the dialogue and encounters created by Stephens himself. In a key departure from the novel, for instance, Christopher's confident assertion that he 'can do anything' is reframed by Stephens as a question; a question that Christopher repeats three times, to be met only with silence from Siobhan.

Christopher's speech may be described as highly idiosyncratic, meaning that his mode of expression is peculiar (distinctive) to him. Christopher's mind is extremely literal, and his use of language reflects this – he very rarely uses figurative language ('The rain looks like white sparks' is a rare example of this [71]) and avoids colloquialisms and slang. He speaks in full sentences and even takes pains to pronounce most words in full, rather than abbreviating or contracting two words together (he will typically say 'do not' rather than 'don't'). Unlike the adults around him, he never swears.

The resulting formality of Christopher's conversation is undercut only by his habit of speaking in long sentences, connecting separate clauses by the conjunctions 'and', 'but' and 'so'. While his sentences are often over-long, however, his use of grammar and syntax (the order of words in a sentence) is always correct. This suggests the speed at which Christopher's mind moves, with thought after new thought flashing through his brain. It also, however, suggests the degree to which Christopher's mind functions by being rigidly methodical, precise and ordered and, by extension, his dependence upon familiar surroundings and routines. If things around him are chaotic or disordered or out of his normal routine, he is easily overwhelmed. When he feels this way, Christopher dispenses with language altogether: he resorts to groaning (as when he is questioned by the police officer, is frightened at Paddington Station or sits his A-Level exam); and retreats into a world of numbers (as when he doubles twos or counts prime numbers) or falls silent.

Things to do

Although some characters only have a small proportion of the play's lines, the way they speak can often convey a great deal about them in relatively few words. Look at how one of the following characters speaks and suggest what it conveys about him or her:

- Mrs Alexander
- Roger
- Reverend Peters

Movement and choreography

Curious Incident has hardly any stage directions. What *Curious Incident* has is problems: it has a series of problems to solve. (2015)

As Stephens attests, stage directions in *Curious Incident* are used sparingly and typically offer very little information as to how a particular scene, or transition, is to be realized: Christopher's epic journey to London, for example, is barely described beyond '*the company dismantle the house. They make Swindon town centre*' (85) and '*the company rebuild and extend and develop the interior of the train*' (93). What these stage directions do tell us, however, is that firstly, the play has been written with a 'company' of actors in mind and, secondly, that the world of the play is to be created *physically*, using the moving bodies of the actors rather than set and props to create the play's various locations. Indeed, Stephens wrote his adaptation with Scott Graham and Steven Hoggett of physical theatre company Frantic Assembly specifically in mind, and movement and dance are integral to the play's realization in performance.[7] Stephens explains this choice:

> The sense I had was the way Christopher thinks, his thinking is balletic. The agility with which he moves from thought to thought is the agility of a dancer, and that lent itself to that physical kind of dance. [These ideas] were an attempt to dramatise [. . .] the interior of Christopher Boone's brain. [I wanted] to get what's *in* there *outside* in his behaviour. (2014)

Marianne Elliott echoes this:

> [We wanted] to make it all look, visually, how his brain might work, and try to get the audience to feel what he feels, emotionally, even though he never articulates emotion, ever. We tried to get the audience inside how he feels about missing his mum in the first half, or inside the hell of that journey in the second half. (2015)

Key passages of the play that were choreographed by Graham and Hoggett include in Part One, Christopher's routine when he comes home from school; Christopher's fantasy about being an astronaut and his memory of his mother in Polperro; and, in Part Two, the extended sequence where Christopher travels from Swindon to London – described by Steven Hoggett as 'the equivalent of an Odyssey . . . almost Homeric in its ambition' (National Theatre Discover, 2012). 'It would make me laugh in rehearsals some days', Luke Treadaway recalls, 'where I'd see the section we were working on might be "Christopher walks into Paddington Station" and, you know,

---

[7] For more information on the work of Frantic Assembly, including its highly acclaimed production of *Othello*, see http://www.franticassembly.co.uk/

it's a week's work of twists and turns and lifts and things'
(National Theatre Discover, 2012).

Music

As physical movement and dance were so central to Stephens
and Elliott's vision for the production, it follows that music
also played a critical role in creating Christopher Boone's
world. The production's composer, Adrian Sutton, reveals how
he created the score for *Curious Incident*:

> Christopher only really likes things that he knows he can
> control – that's why he seeks solace in maths and
> computers, because he knows that they are repeatable and
> have expected results. So it seemed really important that the
> music was also rooted in that concept. It had to be highly
> technological, mathematical, and all very sharp and precise.
> Christopher loves maths and, especially, prime numbers. So
> I thought, okay, let's take the first few prime numbers – 2,
> 3, 5, 7, 11 – and try using them in various ways as applied
> to musical parameters. So, for example, let's make a rhythm
> where the rhythmic emphasis is 2, 3, 5, 7 and 11. So it goes:
>
> **1** 2, **1** 2 3, **1** 2 3 4 5, **1** 2 3 4 5 6 7, **1** 2 3 4 5 6 7 8 9 10 11,
> **1** 2, **1** 2 3, **1** 2 3 4 5 . . .
>
> – emphasizing the downbeats. And that is in fact how the
> show opens, the lights go down and there's a kick drum
> that begins with that rhythm. Another way to apply that
> sequence of numbers is to consider the musical scale as a
> ladder. So you pick the 2nd, 3rd, 5th, 7th and 11th 'step'
> on that ladder and just use those pitches in some way. And
> because neat, ordered, non-random sequences of things
> would appeal to Christopher's brain, it seemed obvious
> that he would want to repeat that sequence of pitches over
> and over. Now you can combine, or stack, those two ideas:
> you can apply the rhythmic emphasis to the pitch model.

When it came to the actual sounds, the actual instruments that played these pitches and rhythms, it seemed again a straightforward decision. As Christopher loves computers, it seemed that all the sounds should be synthetic and computer-generated and pretty much, with one or two exceptions, every sound belongs to this quite mechanistic world, which is what he loves and wants it to be. (2015)

Things to do

1 Try clapping the rhythm described above by Sutton, with the emphasis on the downbeat ('1'). What sort of atmosphere or feeling does this create?

2 If you play a musical instrument, experiment with how you can apply prime numbers to creating pieces of music. What happens, for instance, if you try to make chords from these numbers?

Set and lighting design

Bunny Christie's design for the National Theatre evoked the landscape of Christopher's ordered, methodical mind by seating the audience on four edges of a square playing space, the floor of which resembled mathematical graph paper: white lines forming a glowing grid of tiny squares on a black background. The floor was a blackboard, onto which Christopher could chalk emoticons and diagrams as he tried to deduce Wellington's killer. This space became a virtual map of Christopher's mind, revealing his inner life through lighting and video projections of whirling algebraic equations, galaxies of stars and cascading numbers and letters. Contained within this bare geometric space were secret trap doors, from which 'props were conjured like thoughts from his fevered imagination' (Marmion, 2012) and hundreds of LED lights, which formed 'patterns like [the] neural pathways' of Christopher's brain' (Thompson, 2012). According to Elliott, Christie always knew that 'the set had to be magical, because Christopher's magical. It had to be a magic box and out of this magic box must come these wonderful things. They're hidden, but he thinks of them and, because he thinks of them, they're there' (2015). 'It's a dynamic space', Katy Rudd explains:

> using light, sound, projections and the actors it can quickly be transformed. It's a space where Christopher can just magic or conjure the image that he wants, and then change it straight away: it could be the school but it could also be his home, it could also be Swindon train station. (2015)

Critics were unanimous in their praise for the production's set and lighting design. In her review, Claire Allfree commended 'Christie's exhilarating set' for capturing 'Christopher's perception of the universe as a source of infinite, numeric possibility' (2012).

Critical reception

The following section focuses on the critical response to the 2012 premiere of *Curious Incident* at the National Theatre, London, and its subsequent transfer to the Apollo Theatre in 2013.

Curious Incident was an instant hit with audiences, as witnessed by *Guardian* theatre critic Michael Billington on its opening night: 'It doesn't matter a damn what I or my colleagues say about this adaptation of Mark Haddon's bestselling novel. Last night it was greeted with a roar of approval' (2012). The majority of critics agreed with audiences, commending 'Elliott's fabulously imaginative stagecraft and Luke Treadaway's stunning performance' for its 'vivid visual evocation of how it feels to be inside Christopher's skin' (Brown, 2013): 'The true wonder', declared Susannah Clapp of the *Observer*, 'is that the intimacy of the book – the first-hand knowledge of Christopher's mind – is given real theatrical life' (2012). Stephens's 'funny and extremely moving' adaptation was also highly praised by most critics (Thompson, 2012), with Billington suggesting that the 'play within a play' device 'not only frames the action, but also sets up a rich tension between fictional invention and the obsession with facts, forensics and systemised data that is a symptom of Christopher's autism' (2012). Other reviewers, however, were less convinced, regretting the loss of 'the all-important tonelessness of the novel's first-person narration' (Bassett, 2012). 'The adaptation finds itself staging what is only implied between the lines of a book' wrote Patrick Marmion of the *Daily Mail*, '[Christopher's] world is, therefore less enigmatic and unsettling than it is in the book' (2012). Simon Edge of the *Daily Express* agreed that the device of having Siobhan read out his words 'doesn't work' because 'it gives the boy's unique voice to someone else' but he also conceded that 'what the production loses by diluting Christopher's voice, it makes up for when it shows the very real dilemmas for parents whose love for their disabled [child] is balanced by a terror of not coping' (2012). Billington also praised actors Paul Ritter and Nicola Walker as Christopher's parents, for 'movingly remind[ing] us of the messily contradictory human emotions that co-exist with their son's world of perfect patterns' (2012).

Critics were universal in their praise of Luke Treadaway's 'exceptional' performance as Christopher (Maxwell, 2013). Clapp declared that Treadaway had 'power[ed] himself into another acting realm as Christopher: with his concentrated face and flailing limbs, he is steadily intelligent but physically shaken, mentally agile and emotionally inflexible' (2012). 'Fidgety, annoying and occasionally profound', wrote Henry Hitchings of the *Evening Standard*, '[Christopher] is played with a mixture of grace and feverish intensity by Luke Treadaway. He drools and squirms and groans but mostly his hallmark is a pedantic manner that borders on belligerence. It's a performance of great physical poise and stunning conviction' (2012). Hitchings also credited Steven Hoggett and Scott

Graham's choreographic work with the ensemble, observing that 'it enhances our sense of Christopher's erratic journey through the muddle of relationships' (2012). Clapp was even more enthusiastic with her praise:

> [Frantic Assembly] supply not only their distinctive gymnastic dancing style – characters throw and catch one another, acting as cradles for recumbent actors – but also something more fundamental: a different beat to the action, a beat that goes to heart of Haddon's story. The actors who, swarming, make up a terrifying London crowd, move, perfectly drilled, as a nimble whole; the hero has to teach himself to keep step. This is the wonder of the novel: the ordinary suddenly looks weird; nothing is taken for granted. That is what the stage adaptation gives us again. (2012)

Although widely acclaimed as a 'phenomenal combination of storytelling and spectacle' (Maxwell, 2012), several critics complained of an 'atmosphere marred by self-consciousness and a surfeit of sentimentality' (Evans, 2013), with Matt Wolf of the *International Herald Tribune* describing aspects of the story-telling as 'emotionally rigged' (2012). Michael Coveney of the *Independent* expressed regret that 'the lad trades his rodent Toby for an audience-baiting real-live sweetheart puppy at the end', describing it 'as a grisly sentimental moment' prefigured in the 'cutesy [. . .] toy trains that whizz around the theatre' (2012). While acknowledging that 'the whole thing is done with enormous flair', Billington also found himself resisting 'occasional touches of self-conscious cuteness and sentimentality in Marianne Elliott's production': 'I flinch from manipulative touches such as miniaturised trains and a live dog: two things calculated to send audiences into swooning raptures' (2012). Lyn Gardner of the *Guardian*, however, reviewing the production after its transfer into the West End, offers an alternative perspective:

> There are times when the show comes perilously close to sentimentality, but the clarity of the Christopher's gaze is so

unflinching that it often makes you uncomfortable, and the show is equally clear-eyed on the difficulties of parenting, messiness of life and torment of a child who cannot bear to be touched. The novel gets inside your head, but the stage version does more, giving Christopher's internal response to the world an external manifestation. That world is often a surreal and scary place but oddly beautiful and bizarre too. (2013)

Things to do

Coveney describes the real live puppy that Christopher is presented with by his father as 'audience-baiting'. Billington similarly regards miniature trains and live dogs as 'calculated to send audiences into swooning raptures'. Having diagnosed *Curious Incident* as afflicted by a 'surfeit of sentimentality', Evans archly remarks 'not that the box office is suffering as a result'.

Sentimentality in the theatre is associated with the arousal of feelings or emotions judged too excessive or exaggerated to be sincere: the term holds connotations of extravagance and affectation (performing one's feelings for the benefit of others rather than truly experiencing them) and of letting oneself be led by the frivolous whims of emotion, rather than the clear-sighted judgements of reason. Each of these reviewers makes a link between sentimentality, which they regard with disdain, and popularity with audiences. They suggest that the live puppy and toy train are responsible for 'manipulating' the audience's emotions against their will.

● Do you agree that these production choices are 'manipulative'?

● Why might these critics regard with disdain those aspects of the show that are so popular with audiences?

● Do you think that *Curious Incident* is a sentimental play?

Related work

Stage adaptations of novels

Nicholas Nickleby (David Edgar, 1980)

In their reviews of *Curious Incident* at the National Theatre, a number of theatre critics drew favourable comparisons with the Royal Shakespeare Company's 'gloriously inventive' epic, *Nicholas Nickleby* (Spencer, 2013). Adapted from Charles Dickens's *The Life and Adventures of Nicholas Nickleby* (1838–9), David Edgar's eight and half hour-long stage adaptation premiered at the Aldwych Theatre, London, in 1980. It was presented in two parts and featured a colossal ensemble of thirty-nine performers playing 123 speaking parts in ninety-five scenes. Like *Curious Incident*, Edgar's stage adaptation absorbs a first person narrative into a third person drama (Coveney, 2012). It also adopts the device of onstage narration, presenting a mixture of narrated and enacted scenes, and quotes directly from the novel itself.

The story follows the eponymous hero, left penniless on the death of his father, as he escapes the influence of his villainous Uncle Ralph and embarks on a journey to seek his fortune in 1830s England. Nicholas Nickleby and his loyal companion Smike are played by two actors, supported by an ensemble who multi-role the eccentric characters of Dickens's novel and assemble the novel's various locations, from murky London taverns to open country roads via a prison-like boarding school in Yorkshire from which Nickleby rescues Smike.

Directed by Trevor Nunn and John Caird, the RSC production was highly praised for its theatrical spectacle, with Bernard Levin of *The Times* declaring that 'not for many years has London's theatre seen anything so richly joyous, so immoderately rife with pleasure, drama, colour and entertainment'. An instant success with audiences, the production was filmed for television before transferring to Broadway in 1981.

War Horse (2007); Coram Boy (2005); His Dark Materials (2003)

Curious Incident is not the first successful stage adaptation of a novel produced by the National Theatre in recent years. Director Marianne Elliott was also responsible for the smash hit *War Horse*, adapted by Nick Stafford from the 1982 novel by Michael Morpurgo. Produced in association with Handspring Puppet Company, *War Horse* tells the story of Devonshire-born Albert and his horse, Joey. With the outbreak of World War I, Joey, who Albert trained as a foal, is sold to the cavalry and shipped to the trenches of France. Albert lies about his age, enlists in the army and goes searching for Joey, brought to life in the production by a life-sized, manually-operated mechanical puppet. The production won two Olivier Awards, including Best Theatre Choreography for Toby Sedgwick's 'horse choreography', and, on its transfer to Broadway, six Tony Awards, including Best Play and a Special Tony Award for Adrian Kohler and Basil Jones of Handspring Puppet Company. Other successful stage adaptations for the National Theatre include *Coram Boy*, adapted by Helen Edmundson from the 2000 novel by Jamila Gavin, directed by Melly Still, and *His Dark Materials*, adapted by Nicholas Wright from the fantasy novel trilogy of the same title by Philip Pullman, directed by Nicholas Hytner.

Autism in drama

Motortown (Simon Stephens, 2006)

In 2005, Simon Stephens was writing a play called *Motortown*. He had 'an instinctive sense that at the heart of *Motortown* there [would] be a relationship between a boy and his brother and the brother was going to be autistic', so he read Mark Haddon's novel 'as a general research process to investigate the phenomena of autism' (Stephens, quoted in Ue, 2014: 114). Lee, brother to the play's protagonist Danny, is in his early thirties. He lives independently but receives adult social care in the from of lunches brought to him daily; loves cleaning and ironing and knows the precise population of any capital city across the globe. Like Christopher, he speaks in long but grammatically accurate sentences and has difficulty lying – a trait that leaves Danny, who during the course of the play commits a murder, potentially exposed to the police.

Spoonface Steinberg (Lee Hall, 1999)

Originally written for radio, Lee Hall's *Spoonface Steinberg* premiered at the Crucible Theatre, Sheffield, in 1999. The play is a monologue to be delivered by an actress who plays Spoonface – so named because when she was born 'they looked at my face [and] said it was round as a spoon'. *Spoonface Steinberg* is a meditation on opera, autism, being Jewish and facing death, delivered over a series of arias sung by celebrated opera singer Maria Callas.

Time Spent on Trains (Elizabeth Kuti, 2006)

Time Spent on Trains is a short play for two actors. Jenny, who is '*wearing floaty summer clothes, slightly reminiscent of 1977*', and Peter, who is '*thirty-seven and wears a suit and tie*', sit on a train that has been delayed; Jenny is taking her son to a long-awaited appointment for which they will now be late. Jenny chatters away to Peter, who 'has bare feet' and 'does not look at Jenny, ever'. Peter's responses are limited to repeating scraps of her sentences, the train announcements and half-formed thoughts and phrases. In only eight pages of dialogue, Kuti elegantly dramatizes Jenny's increasingly imploring pleas for Peter to give her 'a sign. To connect us', as well as the profound solace derived from this connection, however fragile or fleeting.

The Six-Days World (Elizabeth Kuti, 2007)

Also by Kuti, *The Six-Days World*, first staged at the Finborough Theatre, London, is a full-length play for six actors, set in a small town in the south-east of England on Christmas Eve, 2007. Eddie returns home to his parents, Ralph and Angela, for the first family Christmas in many years. Neither he nor his parents, however, can forget or forgive themselves for the death of his brother Richard, the memory of whom haunts the drama. The play features an autistic character in the figure of nineteen year-old Tom, whose true relationship to Eddie, Ralph and Angela constitutes the central secret at the heart of this gripping, and extremely moving, family drama.

The Gathered Leaves (Andrew Keatley, 2015)

The Gathered Leaves, which premiered at the Park Theatre, London, in 2015, is also a domestic drama. Several generations of the Pennington family are gathered at the family home to celebrate the seventy-fifth birthday of William Pennington. William uses this opportunity to reveal the fact that he is very ill and making arrangements for his will. Over the course of the bank holiday Easter weekend, other revelations come to light: the breakdown of a marriage, a secret affair, a guilty admission of neglect. The play features an autistic character in forty-nine-year-old Samuel Pennington, who remains immune to the strained relations around him but, when he spills some hot tea, '*bellows*' in '*shock and pain*' and has to be gently coaxed out of his thrashing fit by his brother, Giles. Giles is fiercely protective of Samuel and their relationship emerges as perhaps the most precious and resilient of all relationships in the play.

Glossary of dramatic terms

Act   just as a book is often spilt into chapters, a play is often broken down into a number of units called acts. Each act has its own narrative arc (or structure) and all the acts (depending on the play there may be one, two three or even five acts) combine to provide the narrative arc of the play as a whole. *Curious Incident* is divided into two 'parts' but these serve as the equivalent of acts.

Blocking   deciding where and when the actors will move on the stage.

Character   characters are created to inhabit a writer's work. They may be entirely fictional constructs, or a writer's creative representation of a real or historical figure. Characters in a play are interpreted and performed by different actors every time the play is staged.

Costume   the clothes worn on stage by the characters in a play. Sometimes the playwright will specify or suggest elements of these but even within these stipulations, there will often be a level of creative freedom of interpretation for the designer working on the show.

Director   the person responsible for the overall vision and co-ordination of the production on an artistic level. The director's role includes helping the actors to unlock and interpret elements of character, blocking scenes to ensure all audience members have a good view of the production, and liaising with other members of the creative team, such as designers, to ensure an aesthetically coherent production develops.

Dramatic irony   this is a device by which a playwright draws on knowledge that the audience have, but the characters in the play do not, in order to create dramatic tension. Dramatic irony lies at the heart of *Curious Incident* as we, the reader or audience, understand the social world better than Christopher does. For readers who are familiar with the novel, when Ed tells Christopher that his mother has had to go into hospital because she 'has a problem with her heart' (13), this is a specific moment of dramatic irony.

Lighting   theatres are usually designed to keep out natural light and equipped with the facilities to recreate a range of lighting effects to suit the environments in which a play is set.

Narrative   the way a story is constructed and revealed to its audience or reader is often described by the term narrative. The first part of *Curious Incident* is interesting as an example of a non-linear narrative structure, where events are revealed in a different order from that in which they would have originally happened.

Naturalism naturalism is a style of theatre, usually connected to the work of theatre practitioner Constantin Stanislavski and late nineteenth/early twentieth century playwrights such as Anton Chekhov and Henrik Ibsen. It involves the detailed and realistic representation of life on stage.

Objective what a character wants to achieve at any point in the play; what drives the character.

Playwright the writer of the play. Note the unusual spelling: the term is not play*write* but play*wright*, deriving from the word 'wrought' meaning 'made'. Thus, a playwright is someone who makes plays, as a 'shipwright' is someone who makes ships and a 'cartwright' someone who makes carts.

Props objects used on stage by actors during the course of the play are known as 'props', which is short for 'properties'.

Realism whereas the term 'naturalism' describes a particular movement in theatre, realism is a more general term, which can describe the depiction of many sorts of reality on stage. In other words, a play such as *Curious Incident* might not have a detailed naturalistic set, but it can still incorporate several elements of realism in its depictions of characters and social situations.

Scene the acts of a play can be broken down into smaller units called scenes. These are often differentiated by the time and place of their setting, although scene might sometimes encompass more than one time period or location in order to deliberately contrast events happening in each. The two parts of *Curious Incident* are not formally divided into individual scenes such as 'Act 1, Scene 2', or 'Act 2, Scene Five' and it might be easier to think of them in terms of episodes.

Set the set is the environment that is constructed on a stage for a play to take place within.

Setting the place or places in which the fictional world of the play occurs, which may be represented by the set. Whilst the set is a real space, inhabited by actors, the setting is a fictional space, inhabited by characters.

Sound effect any noise that is deliberately produced in the theatre during the performance of a play. Sound effects may be pre-recorded and mechanically reproduced, or created live by actors or technicians using objects, instruments or their own voices.

Stage direction as well as the lines spoken by the characters, plays contain lines of stage direction, which give instructions to those producing the play.

Subtext there are two ways for dramatists to reveal information about their characters and narrative. They can state information directly and explicitly in the text. For example, a character can tell another character what they are thinking or feeling, or about something that has happened to them in the past. Or, they can use subtext, where a character's dialogue says one thing directly, but may imply or suggest other things, through what is left unsaid or by the way the actor is instructed to say the lines. *Curious Incident* is interesting because Christopher is unable to do anything other than directly state what he is thinking. His use of language is always and completely literal, and he would not understand how to 'imply' or 'suggest' things. Stephens's use of subtext is therefore restricted to his other characters, Ed and Judy in particular. Understanding the subtext behind the text is vital to developing a comprehensive understanding of the play.

Text the text of a play includes its dialogue and stage directions, along with other information provided by the playwright in the form of scene or character descriptions. Sometimes we distinguish between a Written Text, which we read from the pages of a book or script and a Performance Text, which we watch on a stage, and which encompasses a multitude of theatrical elements, such as lighting, costume and imagery. The job of the Written Text is to provide a blueprint from which to create this Performance Text.

CHAPTER TWO

Behind the Scenes

Simon Stephens (playwright)

Simon Stephens is a playwright, and author of the stage adaptation of *The Curious Incident of the Dog in the Night-Time*. He was interviewed by Jacqueline Bolton on 24 July 2015.

JB: How did you approach adapting Mark Haddon's novel for the stage?

SS: One of the things that I was most excited about was physicalizing the people who exist in the novel. Theatre is a behavioural medium, it deals not with what people feel or think or remember or say but with what people *do*. What's extraordinary about the novel is the detail and the energy and the joyfulness and the comedy of Christopher's brain. You read it with empathy and awe because of the way he sees the world. And there's something astonishing about immersing yourself in that perspective for quite a long time. But you can't put what Christopher 'sees' or 'thinks' onstage. It just doesn't work, because 'thinking' is undramatic. So the really hard thing was extricating the play from Christopher's mind. I needed to locate the drama and in order to locate the drama I needed to look at the things that people *do* to each other.

So I did two things. The first thing I did was list all the events that happen in the book. I did this to rid myself of

Christopher's thought process. I just made a list of all the events that happen in the story, so I could remove myself from Mark's gorgeous, intoxicating brain, as filtered through Christopher's voice. And then the second thing I did is notice that Mark is very interesting with his direct speech. He only has people talk to one another out loud, in direct speech, when they're trying to affect each other quite directly. So he actually attributes direct speech like a playwright would. So I went through the novel and I typed out all the direct speech in script form. And had a kind of script which was just everything that any character in the novel says out loud. The play came out of those two documents, and the guiding idea was to make sure everything was behavioural, to make sure everything was active.

The problem, of course, is that you've got to have Christopher's voice in there somewhere because otherwise you miss it. So how do you get Christopher's voice out? I was searching for a kind of narrator. And I became fascinated by the idea that the novel is written as though it is actually a book that a pretend character is writing in a fictional real life. I became really interested in this and it struck me that there are actually only three people who ever read Christopher's book: Christopher, Ed and Siobhan. The problem with Christopher as narrator, however, is that there's no gap, no distance, between what Christopher says and what he feels. There's no dramatic irony or room for interpretation because he just says what he feels all the time. The other two readers, Ed and Siobhan, are more interesting because when they read they *discover*: there's a process of discovery and astonishment in the gesture of them reading Christopher's book. So it creates this quite fascinating dramatic space. When Ed reads the book, it's extraordinary but, if anything, it's actually too dramatic! It's almost too hot because every word he reads kind of breaks his heart. So the story is told mainly through Siobhan, who reads Christopher's story like we read it when we read the book. She has that same sense of joy and awe at Christopher's mind and she also realizes that sometimes things are a bit awry. She knows that Christopher's not got the emotional language to negotiate the pitfalls and perils that face him.

JB: That's interesting, because Siobhan is quite a peripheral character in the novel.

SS: I'm from a family of teachers. My mum was a teacher, my granddad was a teacher, I was a teacher, my cousins are teachers, my nephew's a teacher, my daughter keeps telling me she wants to be a teacher, we just teach in our family. So the notion of teaching has always been very important to me. I also think it is true that everyone has a favourite teacher. Even people who hate school, they have one teacher who gets them a little bit more than the rest. It's a really important relationship in cultures where education is central; it's a really key relationship. So I thought people will really recognize this. They'll remember the one teacher who took time with them, who said to them, 'you're really good at that'. It's such an empowering moment to have someone who gets you in a way that your parents can't get you. And frees you to be yourself, which is what Siobhan does for Christopher. Teaching and theatre are all about bravery, empathy and people realizing their full potential. So it makes sense that a play that has a teacher at the heart of it should be a consideration of those themes.

Marianne Elliott (director)

Marianne Elliott is Associate Director at the National Theatre. She directed the National Theatre premiere of *The Curious Incident of the Dog in the Night-Time* in 2012. She was interviewed by Jacqueline Bolton on 19 August 2015.

JB: Did you anticipate the success of Curious Incident?

ME: You're never really sure if something's going to work. Especially if you want to do something that's slightly out of the ordinary, you're always going into rehearsal with your heart in your mouth, thinking: 'this is a major risk'. I suppose in this instance the stakes were particularly high though, because it is a very well-loved book.

The story is very compulsive, because Christopher is such an unusual individual. And he is very likeable, even though he never tries to be liked – that's never one of his ambitions, ever, which is unusual. There's lots of dramatic irony in the first half, which is always quite compelling to watch, because about mid-way through the first act the audience are beginning to smell that what he thinks has happened to his mother is possibly not the case. And the second half is just an emotional rollercoaster of 'what the hell is he going to happen and how is he going to cope?!' He just goes from one awful frying pan to one awful fire, all the way through the second half.

JB: In performance, *Curious Incident* combines text, physical movement, video projection and music with an incredibly sophisticated set and lighting design. What inspired your ideas for the staging?

ME: We had a week's workshop before we designed the show and that's really really really important for the process. Because when you've only got four weeks rehearsal and then you've got to open – and you're going to be judged, reviews are going to be good or bad – you're in a very particular mental state and you have very little time. When you do a workshop, however, without worrying about the production, you can truly be quite creative and free. So with Scott Graham and Steven Hoggett from Frantic Assembly, we did a lot of experimentation in that week's workshop, exploring how we might create his house, and his street, and his school without any set – I didn't want any set coming on. We didn't have any *time* for a set to come on for five lines, and then the set to go off, and then another set to come on for another five lines in the street. So we explored how we might show the routine of what he does by using physical movement, instead of props or walls or furniture.

One of the things I was very keen on was how to show the poetry of his yearning for his mother, when he remembers her. When he's talking about Polperro and that time he thinks that she died. And I had an image in my head of her being held up by the company and being turned, so you got a sense of how he revered her and how important to him she was. And I wanted to show how she could somersault back into the sea and disappear, as though she had been lost in the water, even though she was just being held up and then falling behind and being hidden by the company standing in front of her. And once we discovered that, we realized that the company could do all sorts of things that, while not realistic, your imagination still went with the idea of it.

We spent a lot of time on the journey to London. We had no idea, absolutely no idea how to do the journey to London. When we got the script it just said something like 'He goes to London', basically. So we have to imagine he's on a train, he's on a tube, he's on a platform . . . how the hell were we going to do that? We spent a lot of time on rhythms, the company creating the rhythm of a train; we spent time sitting in configurations of train carriages; we spent time on creating a busy platform and, since we didn't have that many actors, how we could make this look populated; and how we could make it seem that he was being buffeted about like a pinball machine. So all these things we tried out in the workshop. A lot of things didn't work. A lot of the things that we thought did work, that we thought were so brilliant, didn't work ultimately. But it gave us a sort of language on which we could build the show.

JB: What, in your view, are Christopher's capabilities? How does he develop as the play progresses?

ME: Christopher's capabilities are extraordinary. He's a genius at maths, he's a genius at science, he loves facts and you must only ever say true facts to him, you must never lie. He's extraordinary. But he's also very human, he's a very human person with very human traits: he's very close to us even if we're nowhere near what's called the autistic spectrum. The thing about him is that it is mistaken to believe that he isn't emotional: he is hugely emotional and he feels things just as anybody else does. He just doesn't know how to articulate that, or control or manage or channel that in any way. So that is confusing for him. He doesn't have any guile, he doesn't try to pretend to be anything that he's not, which is what we all try to do all the time.

I think he's hugely underestimated by everybody around him at the beginning of the play and he possibly underestimates himself. I think that he knows, deep down, that the lie he's been fed about his mother is not right. That's why he goes on this detective mission to find out who killed Wellington – I think he's really trying to get to the bottom of this web of lies around him. He therefore gets obsessed about the death of Wellington and that leads him, of course, to finding out about his mum. He develops as a character because I think he starts to realize the complexities of life a bit. He's had quite a mollycoddled, closeted lifestyle, in that he was picked up by the school bus, taken to school, he had his routines, everything was done for him – and suddenly, by being brave, he is a fish out of water. He has to confront so many things, including the complexities of humans. And through all these things I think he does develop. I think the extent to which he can develop, however, is limited and that's what's so important about the last line of the play. It's interesting because a lot of people want to say 'yes' when he asks 'does that mean I can do anything?' But, to me, it would be irresponsible for the production to say that he could do anything because he *can't*. And if the audience go away resolved in their head that he's fine, and isn't he sweet and didn't he do well and now he can do anything – that's just not a realistic view of autism. He can't do anything. He really can't. He's done bloody well but now he's got to live the rest of his life and how difficult is that?

Luke Treadaway (actor)

Luke Treadaway is an actor. He played the role of Christopher in the 2012 National Theatre premiere of *The Curious Incident of the Dog in the Night-Time*. He was interviewed by Jacqueline Bolton on 14 July 2015.

JB: How did you approach playing the role of Christopher?

LT: I think everyone, when they read Mark Haddon's novel, gets a very distinct vision of who Christopher is and what makes him behave the way he does. I think that's the wonderful thing about the book: even if you're not like Christopher you can still find Christopher in yourself, or find yourself in Christopher. The book is about someone who feels that they're different from the world, and they find the world a kind of confusing place. That's a universal thing that I think everyone goes through at least once a day! In terms of preparation, Marianne Elliott told me to go through the book and write down every fact about that character. So, for instance: I like trains, I like dogs, I don't like yellow food, etc. I also had to write down everything that other people say about him; everything that he says about other people; and then draw up a list of questions that I might have about the character. So there were these four columns which mapped out the character, in a sense. Just doing that created this vast list and you realized what a specific kind of person he is, how hard he'd find the world if he had that many struggles with certain things.

So that was part of finding the character, and then a lot of it came through just physically working on different scenes, seeing how you get them to be the most exciting, most rich, complex versions of each moment for Christopher. So, for example, in some scenes you might start out trying to play Christopher like he's very angry, but then you might work out that there's more to be had if you play the scene as if he was just very very curious about it all, or just very very intent on 'detecting'. I think that was the key, really: there's something about Christopher where he wants to follow straight lines – of both movement and of thought. I think he has to operate almost like the grids on the stage, he has to go down one way, turn left, turn right; his mind is quite linear and quite literal in a lot of ways.

JB: Did you conduct much research into autism? How did this inform your acting of Christopher?

LT: I spent a lot of time with Cian Egan, a Youth Patron for the organization Ambitious about Autism, who served as a consultant on the production and has worked with all the subsequent actors who have played Christopher. He's a young guy with Asperger's who is incredibly easy to talk to and very enlightening about what it's like to have Asperger's. I went into schools [Riverside School, Orpington; Southlands School, Lymington; Spa School, south London; and Treehouse School, north London] and talked to people with Asperger's, and the teachers who worked with them. I also read lots of books about it and watched hours of documentaries! So you can do all this detective work and then things start building up and coming together.

But after you've done all that research, at the end of the day he's just *one* guy with autism. You certainly can't try and import all of the information you've gathered and play that through every line or in every scene; it just doesn't work like that. You have to absorb it and let things become part of the landscape that you can mentally walk through as the character. And there are certain ways that your character won't be able to go because of certain mind-sets he has or certain fears and things like that. So you have to let yourself be free and not try to *do* anything or *be* anything; just let the piece and the person breathe through you.

JB: How does Christopher develop through the play?

LT: For Christopher, going from Swindon to London is like you or I going to the moon: an absolutely uncontemplatable journey in length and in how scary it is for him. But he has, and this is often true of people with Asperger's, a very singular focus, an almost obsessive nature, and this lights a fire in him, I think. Also, at the beginning of the play he tells us he's fifteen years, three months and two days old, so he's at that age where he's turning from boy to man, really. And being slightly obsessive or developing a singular focus is true of many teenagers – becoming obsessed with video games, or going out on their skates to the skate park, or whatever it is – it's extremely common in teenagers. So while there are many things that are specific to Christopher, there are also things which just crossover with him and any other teenager of fifteen years old.

I personally think that what he's doing by trying to detect who killed Wellington is, really, trying to work out what happened to his mum. What he is doing from his heart, even though he might not be able to analyse this with his head, is trying to find his mum. That's really what's going on, I think, with the detecting, and I think that's what drives him to go up to London. He certainly grows up a lot in the story and I think that is what's so moving about it: seeing someone struggling so hard but also not backing down; not being broken by different challenges along the way but actually rising to them.

Nick Sidi (actor)

Nick Sidi is an actor. He played the role of Mr Shears in the 2012 National Theatre premiere of *The Curious Incident of the Dog in the Night-Time*. He was interviewed by Jacqueline Bolton on 24 July 2015.

JB: Can you tell me a bit about the workshop with Scott Graham and Steven Hoggett?

NS: To this day, that workshop was the most exciting ten days I've ever had in any rehearsal room, ever. It was totally incredible. I think by the end of the first day there was just this feeling of: we are so lucky, this is so exciting, this is golden. Simon's script was extraordinary; it just punched you in the stomach with its emotional impact. But it was also so *free*, so playful [. . .] With Frantic Assembly, one of the first things we did was this crazy exercise where one person walks slowly into the middle of a group of people, who each takes a piece of that person's body and collectively lifts them. So a person walks and before they know it, they're up in the air. Howard Ward, who was in the show, he's a big strong guy but it was amazing – he could walk in and just by us collectively working together at the same time – whoosh, he would be up in the air. It's amazing how it frees you up, immediately. The barriers come down. Within that first half an hour, as a company, it was like we'd worked together for a year.

Marianne always had this thing of: we're going to tell this story from Christopher's point of view. So how can we show that this is a boy who obviously has rituals, who needs the security of knowing that everything is the same, who doesn't like change – what does he do when he comes home? How can we create Christopher's daily routine? How do we create his room? We were sent off in small groups to create something and we were just constantly trying things. There was no attempt to stage things, no sense of performance or that this was a rehearsal, it was just 'let's see what you can come up with'. 'How do we create his room?', the idea being to use your bodies, to use yourselves as people to create this room. We were doing things like sitting on the floor and pretending to be a toilet so Luke would sit on you, or he would go and open a blind and someone would be there with their hand in the air and Luke would pull something and they would move to the left. And, of course, it's really embarrassing! You're thinking 'what am I doing, some kind of mime?!' But everyone was doing it and everyone was really getting into the spirit of it and, as I say, that freedom we felt was so playful. If you are able to fail, and know that that's okay, that's when a rehearsal room is successful. If you're terrified, or everything is very sacrosanct, I don't think people are as prepared to be ambitious.

And I don't know why, but just something happened, the chemistry of the people in the room was so brilliant. *Curious* explored *physically* what it's like to be Christopher

JB: *Curious* has a very clear protagonist in the character of Christopher but it also features a large ensemble of actors playing lots of different roles. How important was this ensemble to the story and to the production?

NS: We were an ensemble company in the true meaning of the word. Usually if you're in an ensemble then it's a bit like being in a chorus: you get trotted out and you do a big crowd scene and then you're shunted off. We, however, were on stage more or less all the time. We were sitting on plastic boxes at the edge of the playing space, waiting to go into the centre and do stuff. You felt like you were in every moment of every beat. One minute you were sitting on the side and the next you were creating a house. Then you were on the' train. Then you were in the station. And then you were being an actor, saying your lines and playing a character. And the changes, the switches from one moment to the next . . . it was just incredible. It was thrilling. In the Cottesloe [theatre], you could actually hear people gasp. Because one minute you were sitting there, or you were playing a policeman, and within thirty seconds you were lifting somebody up with your hand and spinning him and dropping him back down. And you were two feet away from the audience. It was thrilling to do and exciting to watch. And you were part of that machine, of this incredible company togetherness, and that is *really* what an ensemble is. We all had each other's backs – *physically*. We literally had each other's backs. We were like a family.

Nicola Walker (actress)

Nicola Walker is an actress. She played the role of Judy in the 2012 National Theatre premiere of *The Curious Incident of the Dog in the Night-Time.* She was interviewed by Jacqueline Bolton on 27 July 2015.

JB: What was your experience of working with Frantic Assembly in the workshop for *Curious Incident*?

NW: The biggest thing for all of us, I think, was finding this other way of expressing ourselves, with movement giving us this added physical vocabulary. Because a lot of the time in this country, [acting] is about the script and the words, so to be given a totally different way of acting, a physical way, was fantastic. I think that's probably why all of us are still so emotionally connected to it.

Simon's adaptation, on the first reading, just read brilliantly. Sometimes workshops are about working on the script and you're asked to give your ideas and to say how well you think the script works. I mean that would have been laughable. His script worked absolutely beautifully as it stood that day. But then Marianne sort of pushed away from the table and said 'well, now we have to find how to stage this'. And Scott and Steven were phenomenal because they got us, straightaway, to put our scripts down. In this country it's all about holding the script and arguing about lines and whether you feel your character would do that. But we straightaway put the script down and just started playing with ideas of moving Luke through space, without being able to touch him. We weren't allowed to touch Luke but we were allowed to do things like put him in a plastic box and float him above our heads. Normally in a workshop you're sat down intellectualizing something but Marianne and Frantic went: 'right, we're going to move it physically and see what we can achieve'. And they had all of us flying around the room!

JB: What sort of a character is Judy?

NW: It's interesting, because in the book you only have Christopher's version of his mother and his father. But when you put them on their feet and make them real people they then have their own attitudes that start to bleed through.

Marianne and I started to think about what went unspoken in those letters Judy wrote to Christopher, and what's really underneath some of that positivity and attempt to reach out to her son. And how it would have felt for a mother to send forty-three letters over two years and have nothing back. We always felt that Judy was a really, really good mum doing her best under the circumstances. That she loved her son totally but that the combination of her personality, this very difficult situation with her son, and a marriage that isn't working leads her to take this awful, ridiculous way out that doesn't work. I think she's frightened of not being able to cope. So she takes herself out of that environment and hopes that Christopher will be better off with his dad.

What I like about the end of the play is that it's not bleak, that there is hope in the fact that she's come back. She loves her son so much she realizes that she made the wrong choice. They work as an unusual family unit and, you know, that's better than not having a unit at all. All the shame and self-pity is in there with Judy but her base note is that she really, really loves her son.

On the last day of the workshop, when we seemed to have finished and were packing up, Scott and Steven said 'hang on, we want to do one last exercise'. And they said, 'right, mother and father: you've not been allowed to touch Christopher all this week, so we're going to give you forty-five seconds: you can touch him and look at him and hold him in whatever way you choose'. And the actor playing Christopher's father picked Luke [Treadaway] up like a baby. And they just stood there with him cradling him. He was just holding Luke, he wasn't doing any grand acting, just what he in that moment instinctively felt like doing. A big man, holding another big man. Luke suddenly looked like a baby. And then they said, 'okay, Judy, you've got forty-five seconds'. And what was fascinating was that what Judy seemed to want was *to be held by* Christopher, rather than hold Christopher. So Judy got forty-five seconds to make Christopher hold her, embrace her. And Luke was still being Christopher so he was not actually joining in that embrace. So I was having to hold Luke quite hard, which seemed quite true about Judy, forcing him to love me and to show he loves me and physically touch me and hold me. Because these are all the things that as Judy you don't get to do with Christopher.

Niamh Cusack (actress)

Niamh Cusack is an actress. She played the role of Siobhan in the 2012 National Theatre premiere of *The Curious Incident of the Dog in the Night-Time*. She was interviewed by Jacqueline Bolton on 27 July 2015.

JB: How would you describe Siobhan and Christopher's relationship? What does Siobhan enjoy about Christopher?

NC: I think Siobhan is astounded by his imagination, by his ability to imagine infinity or infinite numbers, because those are the things she can't do. There were times in the play when I felt we were equals because what Christopher had to offer Siobhan she couldn't give to him. And what I could give to him – which was empathy, and engagement and connection – he couldn't offer me. So I think that what she gets is a window into an extraordinary mind. Whereas I think a lot of people meeting Christopher, and indeed his parents, don't get that window. Siobhan gets how his mind works. And can love him and admire him because of that. She sees that he can do stuff she absolutely cannot do and she's thrilled by that. It's like watching a concert pianist play a concerto and you think 'how do you do that'? And I think Christopher's mathematical brain and scientific brain is on a par with a virtuoso musician. The fact that there's another bit of him which isn't developed and can't be developed can, unfortunately, obscure how amazing he is. And I think that is a message in the play: just because a person doesn't express himself or communicate with other people in a typical, 'normal' way, this shouldn't obscure the fact that he is extraordinary. And I think Siobhan absolutely gets that.

I think it's interesting that Marianne chose to cast a middle-aged woman as Christopher's teacher because I think in the book she's younger.[1] Marianne is clearly aware of the dearth of nice parts for women in their middle age. But also, casting a middle-aged woman in the role of Siobhan provides a very interesting challenge to Judy – they could possibly be rival mothers.

JB: What advice would you give to students studying this play?

NC: I think this is a great play to study because it offers opportunities for people to be theatrical, to expand their boundaries as to what a play might be and how you can possibly do a play. This play is more malleable than some other plays, because it allows for a company of actors and playmakers to look at it and say, 'okay, what would you do? How would you solve this problem?' I think that in Stephens's script there's an element of: 'Here's the play: play.' And it's a glorious gift to give to anyone who's interested in making theatre.

---

[1] In Stephens's script, the stage directions state that Siobhan is 'twenty-seven years old' (31).

CHAPTER THREE

Writing About the Play

Although the specific questions asked in examinations will change year on year, overall they will be consistent in asking you to demonstrate certain key skills and knowledge about the text you have studied. For example, you will always need to be able to show that you can:

- Develop an informed personal response to the text. This means that you will need to have your own opinions about the text, but that these must be firmly rooted in the evidence given by the text itself and any additional reading and studying you have done.

- Illustrate your interpretations of the text with appropriate evidence from the text. Choosing the right moments in the play to reference and selecting appropriate quotations from the text is vital if you are to provide a convincing argument in support of your personal response.

- Analyse the key features of the text you have studied, demonstrating how the playwright creates meaning and effect within their work, by examining their use of language, structure and other dramatic techniques.

- Suggest connections between a text and the period in which it was written (its context). You might consider the possible influences of the times on the writer, as well as what the critical, or public, response to the work tells us about its period.

- Maintain an appropriately formal written style throughout your work, using appropriate vocabulary and subject terminology, and standard spelling, punctuation and grammar.

Developing your personal response

It might seem an obvious point, but there is not a lot a Study Guide can tell you about your personal response to a play! This is where it is very important that you allow yourself time to develop your own opinion. There are a number of things you can do to assist this. Most important is reading the text through carefully, but also useful is acting out some of the scenes with friends or classmates so you can experience what it is like to be in each character's shoes. Small or whole group discussions will also help you to develop your ideas about, and responses to, the play. You should never be afraid to contribute to such conversations, or to offer an opinion that is different to those of your classmates, or even your teacher! The whole point of literature and drama is that it is open to multiple interpretations, many of which cannot be considered wholly right or wholly wrong. Of course, some interpretations of the text are more appropriate than others, and listening to other people's views – especially your teacher's – should help you notice alternative ways to consider the text. As a general rule, though, if you can provide evidence from the text to support your interpretation, then that interpretation should be at least partially valid.

You should base your interpretations around three key areas of response:

- The purpose or function of a certain extract or character.

- The thematic significance or 'message' of an extract of text.

- The mood or atmosphere generated within an extract and the possible responses this may provoke from an audience.

Using quotations

When you use a quotation in your work, it is important to be clear about where it comes from and who is saying it so be sure to include where and when the dialogue takes place: 'At school with Siobhan, Christopher describes . . .', for example, or 'When Ed barges into Judy's flat after Christopher has run away, he . . .' Next, you need to make sure the quotation makes the point you want it to, by making this explicitly clear to the reader. This means providing an explanation of what the quotation reveals. For example, you might say something like, 'In this line, Christopher reveals that he is a boy with an exceptionally good memory', or 'Christopher's response demonstrates an inability to understand his mother's feelings'. Whilst you should always explain the value of your quotation in this way, it is not necessary to narrate your own thought process. For example, there is no need to say things like, 'I have chosen this quotation to demonstrate that Christopher has a good memory'; by using the quotation and explaining its value, you make it clear that this is what you have done.

Remember that in an examination, you may have to quote sections of the text from memory. The best way to learn quotations is to act out scenes from the play, so that you gradually learn its lines as an actor would. Although it is best practice to quote the text accurately, if, under the pressure of exam conditions, you cannot remember the exact wording of a line from the text that you want to use, it is better to try to quote what you do remember and get the wording slightly wrong, than not quote at all.

Constructing an argument

To provide a coherent and focused response to an exam or essay question, you need to construct and maintain an argument in response to the question that is being asked. In everyday conversation, the word argument is usually used to describe a disagreement or quarrel, but in academic writing, the word refers to a set of reasons given in support of an idea. An academic argument should provide a combination of reasoning and evidence, which works to persuade the reader or listener of the argument's truth or appropriateness.

The first step towards creating a successful argument is to plan your work thoroughly. You need to think about the point you want to make, and what will be the best way to make it, before you begin writing. In a timed exam, you may feel under a lot of pressure to start writing as soon as your time starts, but taking ten minutes to think through and plan your response to the question is likely to enable you to provide a much clearer and stronger response. Your plan should outline the overall thrust of your argument, as well as the key steps you will need to take you through it. For example, if a question is focused on the relationship between two characters over the course of the play, your plan should identify what you consider the key aspects of this relationship to be, and the scenes, or moments from scenes, that you will draw on to develop and illustrate these aspects.

Well-structured work should also contain a clear introduction, which tells your reader what your essay will discuss, and a succinct conclusion, which sums up the main points of your argument and highlights how they have answered the given question.

Moving from description to analysis

The most straightforward response you can have to a play (or indeed any artwork) is to describe it. This is an important stage in your response to the work, but one that should lead into more developed academic responses, such as analysis and evaluation. Description means saying what you can see, hear or read. For example, you can describe the fact that when Judy goes to hug Christopher, he pushes her away so hard that he falls over. However, this description or observation only really carries any value if you can use it to lead into a point of analysis or evaluation. Analysis means offering a suggestion as to what your description/observation might mean or signify within the context of the play. For example, you might suggest that this moment both reveals Judy's love for her son and reminds us of how hard raising a child with Christopher's needs was for her. Whereas a description is usually unambiguous and objective, an analysis may be more individual; there may be several ways to analyse or interpret the same description. Evaluation means adding a level of critical judgement to your analysis. For example, you might say that Stephens's specification that it is Christopher that falls over, not Judy, is an effective way of communicating how utterly draining the journey from Swindon to London has been for Christopher. Because each of these stages (description, analysis, evaluation) are progressively more subjective and open to multiple interpretations, it is important that you provide evidence to support them.

Connecting text to context

All dramatic and literary texts, indeed all works of art, can be seen as a product of their times. No work is created in such a vacuum, and everything bears traces of its history. It is impossible to appreciate the full value of Stephens's work if you ignore such things as its relation to Mark Haddon's novel or our current understanding of autism and Asperger's Syndrome. However, you should be careful not to over-state such connections, remembering always that the play is a dramatic fiction, not a history book. You can suggest certain influences that may have informed the writer, but you should not claim to know authorial intent, unless you can back this up with a direct quotation.

Ideally, you should refer to elements of context, as and when relevant, throughout your work, rather than in a separate paragraph. Remember that you are trying to demonstrate how context is integrally linked to the play, so it should be discussed in this way, not as something separate that can be disconnected.

Writing with appropriate formality

Written English has a more formal quality than spoken English, so be careful not to lapse into your spoken voice halfway through a piece of written work. Of course, in the play you are studying, characters may speak informally to one another, and use slang and dialect words, which you may draw attention to, using quotations, but your own discussion of the text should maintain a formal tone and standard spelling, punctuation and grammar. Here are some key things to remember:

- Make sure you are always writing in complete sentences, which make full sense and contain a subject (the thing the sentence is about) and a main verb (what you are noting that thing to be doing). For example, 'The play (subject) explores (verb) the world of Christopher Boone.' Be careful not to switch the subject or tense of your sentence half way through.

- Particularly if you have trouble writing with clarity, break your work down into shorter, clearer sentences, rather than running your ideas together into very long ones, which can easily become confusing for the reader.

- Write in paragraphs, starting a new one every time you start to discuss the next key point within your work.

- Take note of the mistakes you are inclined to make by looking over your previous work. If there are spellings you often get wrong, or types of punctuation you struggle to use correctly, the only real solution is to take the time and effort to learn how to use them.

- Writing in the third person can help you express your ideas more succinctly and authoritatively. For example, rather than writing 'I think Judy feels guilty for leaving Christopher' you might write, 'That Judy feels guilty for leaving Christopher is suggested by the number of letters that she writes to him over a two-year period.' The second example is more authoritative because it assumes the reader will agree with the statement without needing to qualify it with the phrase 'I think'. The reader still knows and understands that the following statement is your opinion because they are reading your work, and they are happy to take your word for it, as long as you back the statement up with convincing evidence from the text.

Overall, the best way to develop a clear and formal written style is to read widely and gradually pick up how other writers structure and phrase things. In addition to this you should always try to leave enough time to proof-read your work, as it is easy to make errors, particularly under the pressure of examination conditions.

BIBLIOGRAPHY

Published materials

Bunyan, Paul and Ruth Moore, eds (2013), *The Curious Incident of the Dog in the Night-Time* by Simon Stephens. Methuen Critical Scripts Edition, with teaching activities for Key Stage 3 and GCSE, London: Bloomsbury Methuen.

Haddon, Mark (2003), *The Curious Incident of the Dog in the Night-Time*, London: Random House.

Stephens, Simon (2005), *Plays: One*, London: Methuen.

Stephens, Simon (2011), *Plays: Three*, London: Methuen.

Stephens, Simon (2012), *The Curious Incident of the Dog in the Night-Time*, London: Bloomsbury Methuen.

Stephens, Simon (2015), *The Curious Incident of the Dog in the Night-Time*, Methuen Modern Drama Guide, with commentary by Jacqueline Bolton, London: Bloomsbury Methuen.

Ue, Tom (2014), 'Adapting The Curious Incident of the Dog in the Night-Time: A conversation with Simon Stephens', *Journal of Adaptation in Film and Performance*, 7.1: 113–120.

Theatre reviews

Allfree, Claire, *The Curious Incident of the Dog in the Night-Time* review, *Metro (London)*, 6 August 2012.

Bassett, Kate, *The Curious Incident of the Dog in the Night-Time* review, *Independent on Sunday*, 5 August 2012.

Billington, Michael, *The Curious Incident of the Dog in the Night-Time* review, *Guardian*, 3 August 2012.

Brown, Georgina, *The Curious Incident of the Dog in the Night-Time* review, *Mail on Sunday*, 31 March 2013.

Clapp, Susannah, *The Curious Incident of the Dog in the Night-Time* review, *Observer*, 5 August 2012.

Coveney, Michael, *The Curious Incident of the Dog in the Night-Time* review, *Independent*, 3 August 2012.

Edge, Simon, *The Curious Incident of the Dog in the Night-Time* review, *Daily Express*, 7 August 2012.

Evans, Lloyd, *The Curious Incident of the Dog in the Night-Time* review, *Spectator*, 23 March 2013.

Gardner, Lyn, *The Curious Incident of the Dog in the Night-Time* review, *Guardian*, 14 March 2013.

Hitchings, Henry, *The Curious Incident of the Dog in the Night-Time* review, *Evening Standard*, 3 August 2012.

Marmion, Patrick, *The Curious Incident of the Dog in the Night-Time* review, *Daily Mail*, 10 August 2012.

Maxwell, Dominic, *The Curious Incident of the Dog in the Night-Time* review, *The Times*, 14 March 2013.

Spencer, Charles, *The Curious Incident of the Dog in the Night-Time* review, *Daily Telegraph*, 14 March 2013.

Thompson, Laura, *The Curious Incident of the Dog in the Night-Time* review, *Daily Telegraph*, 4 August 2012.

Wolf, Matt, *The Curious Incident of the Dog in the Night-Time* review, *International Herald Tribune*, 8 August 2012.

Online materials

'Ambitious about Autism', <http://www.ambitiousaboutautism.org.uk/> [accessed 18 August 2015].

Frantic Assembly, <http://www.franticassembly.co.uk/> [accessed 21 August 2015].

Haddon, Mark, 'asperger's and autism', *Mark Haddon*, 16 July 2009, <http://www.markhaddon.com/aspergers-and-autism> [accessed 18 August 2015]

Hoddon, Mark 'Mark Haddon on The Curious Incident of the Dog in the Night-Time', *Guardian*, 13 April 2013, <http://www.theguardian.com/books/2013/apr/13/mark-haddon-curious-incident-book-club> [accessed 18 August 2015].

National Theatre Discover, 'The Curious Incident of the Dog in the Night-Time: working on the spectrum', 2 October 2012, <https://www.youtube.com/watch?v=k2bV75ITXJw> [accessed 20 August 2015].

Theatre Talk, 'The Curious Incident with [sic] the Dog in the Night-Time', 12 November 2014, <https://www.youtube.com/watch?v=3sHa5Zr_iYU> [accessed 20 August 2015].

'The Smarties Tube Test Theory of Mind', *Blethers Speech and Language Therapy*, 9 September 2014, <http://edinburgh-lothian-mobile-speech-therapy.co.uk/news/the-smarties-tube-test-of-theory-of-mind/%E2%80%9D> [accessed 18 August 2015].

Unpublished interviews

Cusack, Niamh, interview with Jacqueline Bolton, London, 27 July 2015.

Elliott, Marianne, telephone interview with Jacqueline Bolton, London, 19 August 2015.

Rudd, Katy, interview with Jacqueline Bolton, London, 24 July 2015.

Sidi, Nick, interview with Jacqueline Bolton, London, 24 July 2015.

Stephens, Simon, interview with Jacqueline Bolton, London, 24 July 2015.

Sutton, Adrian, interview with Jacqueline Bolton, London, 24 July 2015.

Treadaway, Luke, telephone interview with Jacqueline Bolton, 14 July 2015.

Walker, Nicola, interview with Jacqueline Bolton, London, 27 July 2015.

INDEX

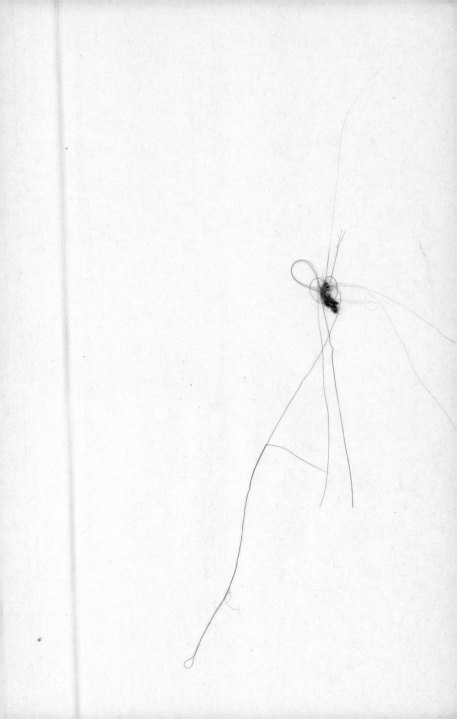